D0212498

THE UNITED STATES AND BRAZIL

OTHER TITLES IN THE
CONTEMPORARY INTER-AMERICAN RELATIONS SERIES
*Edited by Jorge Domínguez
and Rafael Fernández de Castro*

THE UNITED STATES AND MEXICO:
BETWEEN PARTNERSHIP AND CONFLICT

Jorge Domínguez and Rafael Fernández de Castro

THE UNITED STATES AND CHILE:
COMING IN FROM THE COLD

David R. Mares and Francisco Rojas Aravena

THE UNITED STATES AND VENEZUELA:
RETHINKING A RELATIONSHIP

Janet Kelly and Carlos A. Romero

THE UNITED STATES AND ARGENTINA:
CHANGING RELATIONS IN A CHANGING WORLD

Deborah Norden and Roberto Russell

THE UNITED STATES AND PERU:
COOPERATION AT A COST

Cynthia McClintock and Fabián Vallas

THE UNITED STATES AND CARIBBEAN:
TRANSFORMING HEGEMONY AND SOVEREIGNTY

Anthony P. Maingot and Wilfredo Lozano

THE UNITED STATES AND BRAZIL

A LONG ROAD OF UNMET EXPECTATIONS

Mônica Hirst

Conclusion by Andrew Hurrell

ROUTLEDGE

New York • London

Published in 2005 by
Routledge
270 Madison Avenue
New York, New York 10016
www.routledge-ny.com

Published in Great Britain by
Routledge
2 Park Square
Milton Park, Abingdon
Oxon OX14 4RN
www.routledge.co.uk

Routledge is an imprint of the Taylor & Francis Group.
Printed in the United States of America on acid-free paper.

10 9 8 7 6 5 4 3 2 1

Library of Congress Cataloging-in-Publication Data

Hirst, Mônica.
    The United States and Brazil : a long road of unmet expectations / Mônica Hirst ; with
an essay by Andrew Hurrell.
        p. cm. — (Contemporary inter-American relations)
    Includes bibliographical references and index.
    ISBN 0-415-95065-1 (hb : alk. paper) — ISBN 0-415-95066-X (pb : alk. paper)
1. United States—Foreign relations—Brazil.   2. Brazil—Foreign relations—United
States.   I. Hurrell, Andrew, 1955- II. Title. III. Series.
    E183.8.B7H58 2004
    327.73081'09'048—dc22   2004011024

To my parents, Ronny & Zelita

CONTENTS

SERIES PREFACE   ix

INTRODUCTION   xvii

CHAPTER 1   HISTORICAL BACKGROUND   1

CHAPTER 2   NEW COMPLEXITIES IN U.S.-BRAZIL   19
             ECONOMIC RELATIONS

CHAPTER 3   U.S.-BRAZIL POLITICAL RELATIONS   39

CHAPTER 4   BALANCE AND PERSPECTIVES   67

CHAPTER 5   THE UNITED STATES AND BRAZIL: 73
             COMPARATIVE REFLECTIONS
             An essay by Andrew Hurrell

NOTES   109

INDEX   123

The transition from authoritarian rule to constitutional government.

The continentwide economic depression of the 1980s and the subsequent shift toward more open market–conforming economies.

The end of the Cold War in Europe.

The transformation of relations with the United States.

Each of these major events and processes was an epochal change in the history of Latin America and the Caribbean. More striking is that all four changes took place within the same relatively short time, though not all four affected each and every country in the same way. They became interconnected, with change on each dimension fostering convergent changes on other dimensions. Thus, by the beginning of the new millennium, we had witnessed an important transformation and intensification in U.S.–Latin American relations.

This book is part of a series of ten books on U.S. relations with Latin American and Caribbean countries. Each of these books is focused on the fourth of these four transformations—namely, the change in U.S. relations with Latin America and the Caribbean. Our premise is that the first three transformations provide pieces of the explanation for the change in U.S. relations with its neighbors in the Americas and for the changes in the foreign policies of Latin American and Caribbean states. Each of the books in the series assesses the impact of the epoch-making changes upon each other.

The process of widest impact was the economic transformation. By the end of 1982, much of North America, Western Europe, and East Asia launched into an economic boom at the very instant when Latin America plunged into an economic depression of great severity that lasted approximately to the end of the decade. As a consequence of such economic collapse, nearly all Latin American governments readjusted their economic strategies. They departed from principal reliance on import-substitution industrialization, opened their economies to international trade and investment, and adopted policies to create more open market–conforming economies. (Even Cuba had changed its economic strategy by the 1990s, making its economy more open to foreign direct investment and trade.)

The regionwide economic changes had direct and immediate impact upon U.S.–Latin American relations. The share of U.S. trade accounted for by Latin America and the Caribbean had declined fairly steadily from the end of World War II to the end of the 1980s. In the 1990s, in contrast, U.S. trade with Latin America grew at a rate significantly faster than the growth of U.S. trade world-wide; Latin America had become the fastest growing market for U.S. exports. The United States, at long last, did take notice of Latin America. Trade between some Latin American countries also boomed, especially within subregions such as the southern cone of South America, Venezuela and Colombia, the Central American countries, and, to a lesser extent, the Anglophone Caribbean countries. The establishment of formal freer-trade areas facilitated the growth of trade and other economic relations. These included the North American Free Trade Agreement (NAFTA), which grouped Mexico, the United States, and Canada; the Mercado Comun del Cono Sur (Southern Cone Common Market, more commonly known as MERCOSUR), with Argentina, Brazil, Paraguay, and Uruguay; the Andean Community, whose members were Bolivia, Colombia, Ecuador, Peru, and Venezuela; the Central American Common Market (CACM); and the Caribbean Community (CARICOM). U.S. foreign direct and portfolio investment in large quantities flowed into Latin America and the Caribbean, financing the expansion of tradable economic activities. The speed of portfolio investment transactions, however, also exposed these and other countries to marked financial volatility and recurrent financial panics. The transformation in hemispheric international economic relations—and specifically in U.S. economic relations with the rest of the hemisphere—was already far-reaching as the twenty-first century began.

These structural economic changes had specific and common impacts on the conduct of international economic diplomacy. All governments in the Americas, large and small, had to develop a cadre of experts who could negotiate concrete technical trade, investment, and other economic issues with the United States and with other countries in the region. All had to create teams of international trade lawyers and experts capable of defending national interests, and the interests of particular business firms, in international, inter-American, or subregional dispute-resolution panels or "courtlike" proceedings. The discourse and practice of inter-American relations, broadly understood, became much more professional—less the province of eloquent poets, more the domain of number-crunching litigators and mediators.

The changes in Latin America's domestic political regimes began in the late 1970s. These, too, would contribute to the change in texture of inter-American relations. By the end of the 1990s, democratization based on fair elections, competitive parties, constitutionalism, and respect for the rule of law and the liberties of citizens had advanced and was still advancing throughout the region—albeit unevenly and with persisting serious problems, Cuba being the principal exception. In 2000, for example, for the first time since their revolution, Mexicans elected an opposition candidate, Vicente Fox, to the presidency, and Alberto Fujimori was compelled to resign in Peru, accused of abuse of power, electoral fraud, and corruption. In each instance, the cause of democratization advanced.

Democratization also affected the international relations of Latin American and Caribbean countries, albeit in more subtle ways. The Anglophone Caribbean is a largely archipelagic region, long marked by the widespread practice of constitutional government. Since the 1970s, Anglophone Caribbean democratic governments rallied repeatedly to defend constitutional government on any of the islands where it came under threat and, in the specific cases of Grenada and Guyana, to assist the process of democratization in the 1980s and 1990s, respectively. In the 1990s, Latin American governments also began to act collectively to defend and promote democratic rule; with varying degrees of success and U.S. support, they did so in Guatemala, Haiti, Paraguay, and Peru. Democratization had a more complex relationship to the content of specific foreign policies. In the 1990s, democratization in Argentina, Brazil, Uruguay, and Chile contributed to improved international political, security, and economic relations among these southern cone countries. Yet, at times, democratic politics made it more difficult to manage international relations over boundary or territorial issues between given pairs of countries, including Colombia and Venezuela and Costa Rica and Nicaragua. In general, democratization facilitated better relations between Latin American and Caribbean countries on the one hand, and the United States on the other. Across the Americas, democratic governments, including the United States and Canada, acted to defend and promote constitutional government. Much cooperation over security, including the attempt to foster cooperative security and civilian supremacy over the military, would have been unthinkable except in the new, deeper democratic context in the hemisphere.

At its best, in the 1990s, democratic politics made it possible to transform the foreign policies of particular presidential administrations into the foreign policies of states. For example, Argentina's principal political parties endorsed the broad outlines of their nation's foreign policy, including the framework to govern much friendlier Argentinean relations with the United States. All Chilean political parties were strongly committed to their country's transformation into an international trading state. The principal political parties of the Anglophone Caribbean sustained consistent, long-lasting foreign policies across different partisan administrations. Mexico's three leading political parties agreed, even if they differed on specifics, that NAFTA should be implemented, binding Mexico to the United States and Canada. And the administrations of George H. W. Bush and Bill Clinton in the United States followed remarkably compatible policies toward Latin America and the Caribbean with regard to the promotion of free trade, pacification in Central America, support for international financial institutions, and the defense of constitutional government in Latin America and the Caribbean. Both administrations acted in concert with other states in the region and often through the Organization of American States. Democratic procedures, in these and other cases, establish the credibility of a state's foreign policy, because all actors would have reason to expect that the framework of today's foreign policy would endure tomorrow.

The end of the Cold War in Europe began following the accession in 1985 of Mikhail Gorbachev to the post of general secretary of the Communist Party of the Soviet Union. The end accelerated during the second half of the 1980s, culminating with the collapse of communist regimes in Europe between 1989 and 1991 and the breakup of the Soviet Union itself in late 1991. The impact of the end of the U.S.-Soviet conflict on the hemisphere was subtle but important: the United States was no longer obsessed with the threat of communism. Freed to focus on other international interests, the United States discovered that it shared many practical interests with Latin American and Caribbean countries; the latter, in turn, found it easier to cooperate with the United States. There was one exception to this "benign" international process. The United States was also freed to forget its long-lasting fear of communist guerrillas in Colombia (who remained powerful and continued to operate nonetheless) in order to concentrate on a "war" against drug trafficking, even if it undermined Colombia's constitutional regime.

The process of ending the Cold War also had a specific component in the Western Hemisphere—namely, the termination of the civil and international wars that had swirled in Central America since the late 1970s. The causes of those wars had been internal and international. In the early 1990s, the collapse of the Soviet Union and the marked weakening of Cuban influence enabled the U.S. government to support negotiations with governments or insurgent movements it had long opposed. All of these international changes made it easier to arrange for domestic political, military, and social settlements of the wars in and around Nicaragua, El Salvador, and Guatemala. The end of the Cold War in Europe had an extraordinary impact on Cuba as well. The Cold War did not end the sharp conflict between the U.S. and Cuban governments, but the latter was deprived of Soviet support, forcing it to recall its troops overseas, open its economy to the world, and lower its foreign policy profile. The United States felt freer to conduct a "Colder War" against Cuba, seeking to overthrow its government.

Two other large-scale processes, connected to the previous three, had a significant impact in the international relations of the Western Hemisphere. They were
the booms in international migration and cocaine-related international organized
crime. To be sure, migration and organized crime on an international scale in the
Americas are as old as the European settlement begun in the late-fifteenth century and the growth of state-sponsored piracy in the sixteenth century. Yet the
volume and acceleration of these two processes in the 1980s and 1990s were truly
extraordinary.

Widespread violence in Central America and Colombia, and economic depression everywhere, accelerated the rate of emigration to the United States. Once
begun, the process of migration to the United States was sustained through
networks of relatives and friends, the family-unification provisions of U.S.
legislation, and the relatively lower costs of international transportation and
communication. By the mid-1990s, over twelve million people born in Latin
America resided in the United States; two-thirds of them had arrived since 1980.
The number of people of Latin American ancestry in the United States was even
larger, of course. In the 1980s, migrants came to the United States not just from
countries of traditional emigration, such as Mexico, but also from countries that
in the past had generated few emigrants, such as Brazil. As the twentieth century
ended, the United States had become one of the largest "Latin American" countries in the Americas. The United States had also come to play a major role in the
production and consumption of the culture—including music, book publishing,
and television programming—of the Spanish-speaking peoples. All of these
trends are likely to intensify in the twenty-first century.

Had this series of books been published in the mid-1970s, coca and cocaine
would have merited brief mention in one or two of the books, and no mention in
most of them. The boom in U.S. cocaine consumption in the late 1970s and 1980s
changed this. The regionwide economic collapse of the 1980s made it easier to
bribe public officials, judges, police, and military officers. U.S. cocaine supply interdiction policies in the 1980s raised the price of cocaine, making the coca and
cocaine businesses the most lucrative in depression-ravaged economies. The generally unregulated sale of weapons in the United States equipped gangsters
throughout the Americas. Bolivia and Peru produced the coca; Colombians grew
it, refined it, and financed it; criminal gangs in the Caribbean, Central America,
and Mexico transported and distributed it. Everywhere, drug traffic–related
violence and corruption escalated.

The impact of economic policy change, democratization, and the end of the
Cold War in Europe on U.S.–Latin American relations, therefore, provide important explanations common to the countries of the Americas in their relations
with the United States. The acceleration of emigration, and the construction and
development of international organized crime around the cocaine business, were

also key common themes in the continent's international relations during the last two decades of the twentieth century. To the extent pertinent, these topics appear in each of the books in this series. Nonetheless, each country's own history, geographic location, set of neighbors, resource endowment, institutional features, and leadership characteristics bear as well on the construction, design, and implementation of its foreign policy. These more particular factors enrich and guide the books in this series in their interplay with the more general arguments.

As the 1990s ended, dark clouds reappeared on the firmament of inter-American relations, raising doubts about the "optimistic" trajectory that seemed set at the beginning of that decade. The heavy presence of the military on civilian society was significantly felt in Colombia, Venezuela, and Peru (until the end of Alberto Fujimori's presidency in November 2000). In January 2000, a military coup overthrew the constitutionally elected president of Ecuador, although the civilian vice president soon reestablished constitutional government. Serious concerns resurfaced concerning the depth and durability of democratic institutions and practices in these countries. Venezuela seemed ready to try once again much heavier government involvement in economic affairs. And the United States had held back from implementing the commitment to hemispheric free trade that both presidents George H. W. Bush and Bill Clinton had pledged. Only the last of these trends had instant international repercussions, but all of them could affect adversely the future of a Western Hemisphere based on free politics, free markets, and peace.

THIS PROJECT

Each of the books in the series has two authors, typically one from a Latin American or Caribbean country and another from the United States (and, in one case, the United Kingdom). We chose this approach to facilitate the writing of the books and ensure that the books would represent the international perspectives from both parts of the U.S.–Latin American relationship. In addition, we sought to embed each book within international networks of scholarly work in more than one country.

We have attempted to write short books that ask common questions to enable various readers—scholars, students, public officials, international entrepreneurs, and the educated public—to make their own comparisons and judgments as they read two or more volumes in the series. The project sought to foster comparability across the books through two conferences held at the Instituto Tecnológico Autónomo de México (ITAM) in Mexico City. The first, held in June 1998, compared ideas and questions; the second, held in August 1999, discussed preliminary drafts of the books. Both of us read and commented on all the manuscripts; the manuscripts also received commentary from other authors in the project. We also hope that the network of scholars created for this project will continue to function, even if informally, and that the webpage created for this project will provide access for a wider audience to the ideas, research, and writing associated with it.

We are grateful to the Ford Foundation for its principal support of this project and to Cristina Eguizábal for her advice and assistance throughout this endeavor. We are also grateful to the MacArthur Foundation for the support that made it possible to hold a second successful project conference in Mexico City. The Rockefeller Foundation provided the two of us with an opportunity to spend four splendid weeks in Bellagio, Italy, working on our various general responsibilities in this project. The Academic Department of International Studies at ITAM hosted the project throughout its duration and the two international conferences. We appreciate the support of the Asociación Mexicana de Cultura, ITAM's principal supporter in this work. Harvard University's Weatherhead Center for International Affairs also supported aspects of this project, as did Harvard University's David Rockefeller Center for Latin American Studies. We are particularly grateful to Hazel Blackmore and Juana Gómez at ITAM, and Amanda Pearson and Kathleen Hoover at the Weatherhead Center, for their work on many aspects of the project. At Routledge, Melissa Rosati encouraged us from the start; Eric Nelson supported the project through its conclusion.

Jorge I. Domínguez
Harvard University

Rafael Fernández de Castro
ITAM

Relations between the United States and Brazil entered the twenty-first century facing new challenges and opportunities. Major transformations in the substance and format of bilateral ties have been connected to new landscapes in the domestic and international affairs of both countries. The combination of outstanding economic performance with an unchallenged military primacy and political leadership has allowed the United States to reaffirm hegemonic attributes, becoming the most powerful actor in the world power system. For Brazil, the impact of democratization, together with the effects of world economic globalization and the end of the Cold War, redesigned domestic and external pressures and interests. Nowadays, Brazil seeks a positive agenda with the United States, though the texture of this relationship has become more complex and difficult to categorize under a single label. The post–Cold War world poses new challenges and opportunities for the United States and Brazil. Thus, new areas of convergence and of discrepancies between the two countries have emerged, introducing new flavors to the main course.

U.S.-Brazil relations have gone through different phases, oscillating from "good" to "cool" without ever experiencing hostility, making such relations unique in the Western Hemisphere. While Mexico has carried the burden of war and territorial loss to the United States, Argentina is still "making up" for the strong anti-American sentiments that shaped its foreign policies through most of the twentieth century.

Brazil and the United States have shared a notion of "constrained discrepancy" which, while it has always avoided open confrontation, has resulted in frustrations on both sides that have long dominated their relations. U.S.-Brazil relations have faced cyclical crises of expectations caused by erroneous calculations on both sides. At the end of World War II, Brazil expected special acknowledgment for having fought against the Axis powers. New frustrations emerged in the early 1950s, when the Brazilian government was not granted support for its economic development policies; in the mid-1960s, when it did not receive economic compensation for having contained "domestic communist forces"; and in the mid-1970s, first for not having been upgraded as a key country for U.S. foreign policy and then later for having been included as one of the target countries for U.S. nonproliferation and human rights policies. In the mid-1980s Brazil, together with other Latin American countries, regretted the U.S lack of a political approach in dealing with the debt crisis and, in the mid-1990s, the lack of support in a period of global financial turmoil.

The frustrations have also cumulated on the U.S. side. While Brazil's nationalist economic policies have bothered U.S. economic interests since the 1950s, Brazil's resistance to align militarily with the United States during the Korean War in the 1950s, the Vietnam War in the 1960s, the U.S. Central American policy of the 1980s, and the Persian Gulf War in the 1990s has upset U.S. administrations from time to time. The U.S. government has also become uncomfortable with Brazil's foreign policy management, which was centralized under its Foreign Ministry.

Nevertheless, throughout the twentieth century bilateral relations have played a crucial role in Brazil's foreign affairs as well as in the U.S. hemispheric agenda. They have evolved throughout different phases: the first was labeled an (unwritten) *alliance* that was shaped as Brazil became a republic and lasted until the early 1940s; the second is characterized by Brazilian *alignment* to the United States, starting in 1942 and ending in 1977; in the third Brazil assumed an *autonomous* policy toward the United States, which it maintained until 1990, when it inaugurated a phase of *adjustment* regarding U.S. relations that combined a more flexible posture vis-à-vis U.S. expectations with previous premises of an autonomous foreign policy. More recently, since the inauguration of the government of Luiz Inácio Lula da Silva (January 2003) in Brazil, an *affirmative* posture has slowly been taking form in U.S.-Brazil relations.

Although U.S.-Brazil relations have always been dominated by an intergovernmental agenda, nongovernmental actors have recently expanded their presence dramatically. Besides a diversified set of economic interests, nongovernmental organizations are now part of a lively bilateral interaction. Hence, U.S.-Brazil relations have become more complex on both sides: intergovernmental difficulties coexist with an open agenda in which military, economic, political, and cultural forces have introduced new concerns and interests. The main purpose of this book is to portray this reality.

This book aims to cover the many issues and areas that shape U.S.-Brazil relations, first through a brief historical overview and then through an updated analysis of interstate and intersocietal ties. It has been structured into five parts. Following this brief introduction, chapter 1 addresses the historical evolution of

U.S.-Brazil relations through the end of the twentieth century. Chapter 2 analyzes the new complexities of U.S.-Brazil economic relations by focusing on three specific dimensions: relations regarding Brazilian economic policies, commercial transactions, and bilateral relations in the context of regional trade negotiations. Chapter 3 examines the political relations between the two countries. The *first tier* issues are primarily addressed from an interstate platform, such as world and regional politics and security, while *second tier* issues are led by nongovernmental actors, and address such issues as human rights, the environment, Brazilian immigration to the United States, and public opinion. To conclude, chapter 4 lays out some perspectives for U.S.-Brazil relations for the near future. Chapter 5, an essay by Andrew Hurrell, "The United States and Brazil: Comparative Reflections," follows.

I am very thankful for the assistance of Maria Rivera and Ximena Simpson. I would also like to express my gratitude to Jorge Domínguez, Rafael Fernández de Castro, and Maria Regina Soares de Lima for their extremely helpful comments and suggestions. It is important to note my gratitude that this volume could include an essay written by Andrew Hurrell from the "non-Brazilian" viewpoint of U.S.-Brazil relations. Additionally, I would like to thank Donald Halstead for his editorial suggestions. Finally, despite the generous assistance I have received, I alone bear responsibility for whatever errors and inconsistencies might remain in the work presented herein.

HISTORICAL
BACKGROUND

Relations between the united states and brazil have ebbed and flowed over time; for almost two hundred years they have oscillated between close alignment and cold indifference, according to the level of convergence and/or discrepancy between the two countries. Yet their shared American heritage, together with their power attributes—territory, population, and size of economy—have always made it difficult for either side to turn a blind eye to the other.[1]

Until the late nineteenth century, relations between the two countries were sporadic, as was then the norm in inter-American relations. Their dominant ties were with the European world—particularly with Great Britain—and wars and border settlements occupied almost all of the foreign agendas of the two countries.

U.S.-Brazil relations gained weight as bilateral economic and political interests gradually flourished in the last decade of the nineteenth century. While Brazilian republican movements looked to the U.S. political experience as a source of inspiration, the United States opened its market to coffee, Brazil's main export. The relationship picked up once Brazil abolished slavery and became a republic. Since then, U.S.-Brazil relations have developed different significant trends, which will now be discussed individually.

ALLIANCE

During Brazil's First Republic (1889–1930), U.S.-Brazil relations followed the pattern of a loose alliance, one that Bradford Burns has characterized as an "unwritten alliance."[2] While no mutual military assistance was involved, reciprocal diplomatic support and close economic ties knitted a strong friendship between the two nations. For Brazil, this relationship was premised on the diagnosis of a scenario in which Eurocentric interests would not last long as the core of world affairs, and the United States would become a vigorous international actor. Barão de Rio Branco, foreign minister (1902–12) and founding father of twentieth-century Brazilian diplomacy, was the main architect of this conception.

Nevertheless, it is important to keep in mind that the idea of giving preference to the strengthening of relations with the United States was conceived in a multipolar world system, and was based upon the belief that it would be more likely that this structure would experience relevant adjustments than a complete collapse. In other words, Brazil's relations with the United States did not anticipate the constraints that latter would be imposed by U.S. hegemony. Hence, in those days, Brazil and the United States basically met each other's expectations.

The First Republic (1889–1930) was a decisive era for Brazil in the diplomatic arena, and essential premises instituted during this period still provide a necessary backdrop for understanding contemporary Brazilian foreign policy. It was at this time that Brazil's Foreign Ministry affirmed its position as the dominant actor in formulating and conducting Brazil's foreign affairs. Following the settlement of most long-standing territorial disputes with its South American neighbors, Brazil began to exhibit greater interest in engaging in multilateral diplomacy and developing closer ties with the United States. At this time, the United States was perceived as the ascendant power in the international system. Hence, at the turn of the nineteenth century, as Brazil gradually distanced itself from the British sphere of influence, U.S.-Brazil relations began to flourish. Early U.S. support for Brazil's provisional government, established in 1889, helped solidify the relationship. The Treaty of Commercial Reciprocity (1891) augmented existing commercial ties between the two nations, as did the subsequent U.S. naval presence off the Brazilian coast.[3]

Throughout the First Republic, Brazil hoped to crystallize its alliance with the United States, which praised the settlement of the border disputes between Brazil and Argentina, and supported Brazil in its territorial negotiations with British and French Guyana. Brazil reciprocated when it supported the U.S. government politically and logistically during the 1898 war with Spain. The two countries continued to cultivate diplomatic relations, as evidenced by the inauguration of their respective embassies in each other's capitals. Most telling of all is the fact that the U.S. embassy in Rio de Janeiro was the first that the United States opened anywhere on the entire South American continent, while the Brazilian embassy in Washington, D.C., was Brazil's first embassy abroad.

The years of Rio Branco at the Foreign Ministry were crucial for the creation of the special relationship with the United States. Both Rio Branco, as foreign minister, and Joaquim Nabuco, as ambassador, worked hard to assure that the United States showed goodwill toward the governments of the First Republic.

Rio Branco was especially concerned with consolidating harmonious relations with the most prominent partner in the Americas, but he believed close relations with the United States should not overshadow other alliances in the region, particularly the alliance with Argentina. Hence, Rio Bronco's idea of creating an entente among Brazil, Argentina, and Chile did not exclude the maintenance of close relations with the United States. Later, U.S. support for Brazilian naval rearmament (1913) was reinforced by negotiations in 1922 for a cooperative military program.

Positive bilateral relations during the First Republic, however, did not preclude some divergence in diplomatic stance between the two. For instance, the United States and Brazil stood for different viewpoints in the Second Hague Peace Conference (1907), on the division of Colombia and the consequent creation of Panama, and on certain trade negotiations. Furthermore, "dollar diplomacy," which led to continuous U.S. interventions in Latin America, fed a growing controversy within Brazilian diplomatic and political circles on the pros and cons of close relations with the United States.

In the early twentieth century, trade relations with the United States were crucial for Brazil, but they were highly asymmetrical from the start. Between 1910 and 1914, for instance, 38 percent of Brazilian exports were geared toward the United States, whereas a mere 1.5 percent of U.S. exports were destined for Brazil. After World War I, U.S. exports to Brazil grew substantially,[4] and the United States became a leading investor in Brazil, especially after the expansion of transportation and mining. At the time, a decrease in the number of British firms in Brazil correlated with an increased U.S. presence.

This picture began to change in the mid-1930s, when U.S. expectations regarding Latin American economic and political loyalty increased. Brazil's 1930 revolution paved the way for major political and economic transformations that reflected on its relations with the United States. The 1930s can be considered a transition period in U.S.-Brazil relations. The new civil and military elite that came to power deepened the link between foreign affairs and domestic economic policies, and growing international tensions, coupled with major changes in the domestic affairs of both Brazil and the United States, engendered a unique situation for the relationship. While German influence expanded in Brazil, the United States pushed for the intensification of economic, political, and cultural ties with all Latin American countries, particularly Brazil. This effort was carried forward in the framework of the "good neighbor policy."

In this context, Brazilian foreign affairs became increasingly influenced by the commercial options posed by the U.S.-German rivalry. Whereas the United States insisted on free trade, Germany offered Brazil the advantages of compensated trade. The administration of Getúlio Vargas (1930–45) pragmatically analyzed the benefits of an expanded relationship with Germany at the cost of Brazil's traditional partnership with the United States, while it tried to extract maximum advantages from relations with both countries.[5]

With the strengthening of industrial interests, an internal debate over foreign economic policy surfaced. In 1935, a controversy arose regarding the trade agreement negotiated with the United States in that same year. Following the liberal principles of U.S. economic policy, this treaty established the reciprocal concession of Most Favored Nation status. It also considered preferential treatment for some Brazilian products (coffee, cocoa, and rubber, among others) in exchange for tariff reductions ranging from 20 percent to 60 percent on industrial products such as machines and stainless steel. The political difficulties facing the treaty's approval in Brazil generated a great deal of apprehension in the United States, which was worried about Brazilian protectionism and the country's increased trade with Germany. The Brazilian Congress finally ratified the agreement in 1936.

Oswaldo Aranha, first as Brazilian ambassador to Washington (1934–37), and later as foreign minister (1938–44), advocated the political and economic advantages of deepening relations with the United States. In order to sustain this position, negotiations were undertaken with the U.S. government for the financing of a Brazilian national steel plant and for the modernization of the Brazilian armed forces. Thus, the economic, military, and cultural connections between the two nations were strongly reinforced.

But the onset of World War II in 1939 highlighted the stakes surrounding alignment with the United States. Hoping to conserve an equidistant position vis-à-vis the Allies and the Axis powers, Brazil initially declared its neutrality. Notwithstanding, this commitment to neutrality proved illusory. U.S. involvement in World War II immediately increased pressure from Washington for Latin American alignment. In the case of Brazil, full support was deemed necessary not only for political reasons but because of the strategic importance of Brazil's northeastern coast during the first phase of the war. In August 1942, after a complex process of negotiations, Brazil's alignment with the United States was fully achieved.

While the decline of Brazilian trade with Germany as a consequence of the U.S. naval blockade had circumscribed Vargas's bargaining power, henceforth he would capitalize on his newly acquired leverage by committing Washington to Brazil's economic development. The pro-U.S. sectors were willing to completely give up trade with the Third Reich on the condition that the United States establish a "special relationship" with Brazil, involving deep economic and military cooperation. The new terms of the U.S.-Brazil relationship would accompany Brazil's decision to break off relations with the Axis powers. For Vargas, it was essential that Brazil be compensated for its concessions to the United States via the reequipping of its armed forces.[6] Pro-U.S. solidarity oriented Brazil's actions during the Third Meeting of Consultation of American Foreign Ministers, which took place in January 1942 and also resulted in the decision by the Latin

American nations—with the exception of Argentina and Chile—to break off relations with the Axis powers.

The 1942 Washington Agreements, in which the United States offered Brazil a 100-million-dollar loan for the aforementioned steel plant, met previous expectations. Moreover, the two countries signed a secret military accord, and Brazil authorized the installation of a U.S. naval base within its territory. Finally, in August 1942, Brazil declared war against Germany and Italy. U.S. president Franklin D. Roosevelt's visit to the naval base at Natal in January 1943 highlighted the importance of Brazilian support for the United States, while Roosevelt's meeting with Vargas marked the apogee of wartime rapprochement between the two nations.

Brazil was the only Latin American country to send troops to Europe during World War II, and its expectations for acknowledgment were high. As Brazil perceived itself to be an "associate power" in the struggle, it assumed it would deserve a prestigious position in the postwar peace conferences. However, these expectations turned into frustration as the Brazilian government realized that U.S. postwar priorities were directed toward Europe instead of compensating its closer Latin American fellows.

ALIGNMENT

With a few exceptional periods, U.S.-Brazil relations from 1942 until 1974 followed the pattern of the wartime relationship. Until the late 1960s Brazilian support was a useful tool for the U.S. efforts to first establish and then maintain the Inter-American System. Yet the United States focused its attention on European reconstruction, leaving little room for Latin American, and particularly Brazilian, expectations of a new position in the global diplomatic arena.

In spite of its resentment of the lack of acknowledgment for its cooperation, Brazil stuck to an anti-Soviet diplomacy that completely converged with U.S. political and military expectations. Even though Brazilian foreign policy during the administrations of Jânio Quadros and of João Goulart (1961–64) attempted to break out from U.S. ideological dominance, alignment had become the main option of coexistence with the United States. From the beginning of the Cold War, Brazil invariably supported the United States in international political forums. Alignment with Washington coincided with Brazil's strong ideological identification with Western values and anticommunism and led to a consistent anti-Soviet foreign policy that Brazil also adopted toward other countries within the USSR's sphere of influence.

Washington was able to rely on Brazil's full support in the initial buildup of the Inter-American System. Brazil acted as a special ally of the United States at the 1947 Rio de Janeiro Conference, where the Inter-American Treaty of Reciprocal Assistance was signed, and at the 1948 Bogotá Conference, where the Organization of American States (OAS) was created.

Meanwhile, military cooperation between the two countries expanded, as did U.S. influence in Brazilian military training and defense doctrine. The most notable examples of this were the 1946 institution of the Joint Heads of Staff and the creation of a war college modeled on the U.S. National War College in Washington. Hemispheric security doctrines were absorbed into national security policies.

Brazil also gave its political support to the United States throughout the Korean War. In 1949, Brazil recognized the government of the Republic of Korea (South Korea) and later endorsed a U.S.-led resolution condemning the People's Republic of China for its invasion of Korea. However, the Vargas government was not able to obtain congressional approval to send troops to Korea as had been requested by U.S. president Harry Truman. Brazil had hoped to obtain economic compromises from the United States in exchange for political loyalty, but the U.S. administration of Dwight D. Eisenhower (1953–62) was reluctant to provide funds for development projects in the Bank for International Recovery and Development (BIRD) and in the U.S. Export and Import Bank (Eximbank). Hence, U.S.-Brazil economic relations were essentially limited to trade.

Despite recurrent disappointments regarding economic cooperation, Brazil's strategic compromises to the United States remained unaltered; their military ties continued to be active, and Brazilians remained loyal to the ideological premises of U.S. security doctrine. In this context, negotiations for the installation of a U.S. missile-watch post on the island of Fernando de Noronha were completed in 1957. The two countries also signed an agreement for the civil use of atomic energy, which involved the supply of American uranium for Brazilian nuclear reactors.

Slowly, Brazilian diplomacy started to become less dogmatic regarding the East-West divide. Brazilian relations with the Soviet Union gradually thawed, and commercial ties between the two nations were reestablished in 1959. At that time, Brazil's president Juscelino Kubitschek assumed new foreign policy postures regarding economic development. Cognizant of Brazil's position within the U.S. sphere of influence, Kubitschek advocated the importance of economic cooperation in the context of hemispheric affairs and promoted the Pan-American Operation, which was launched in 1958. This initiative's most important recommendations were increased investment and technical assistance programs for the region, minimum prices for commodities, and the support of multilateral financial institutions for development programs. The proposal was sponsored by Brazil together with Argentina and had the support of most countries in South America.

The Cuban revolution gave the United States renewed legitimacy in strengthening containment policies in the Americas, which immediately minimized the impact of the Pan-American Operation. In this context, the administration of

John F. Kennedy (1961–63) announced the Alliance for Progress, its own program of economic assistance to redress Latin America's concerns.

A broad renewal of the premises of Brazil's foreign policy took place under the administrations of Jânio Quadros (1961) and João Goulart (1961–64). Called at the time the Independent Foreign Policy, it reviewed all aspects of Brazilian foreign affairs with the aims of expanding the country's autonomy in the international arena and reducing the constraints imposed by the bipolar international order. Brazil's foreign affairs needed to be motivated by its own national interests and not by the pressures of the United States or other great powers; it was therefore necessary for Brazil to diversify and deepen its external political and economic ties.

The United States did not welcome the new stance of Brazil's foreign policy, especially when it tried to keep a more independent position toward the Cuban revolution. This lack of sympathy toward Brazil's policy increased even more when Goulart's government enforced nationalistic economic policies that hurt the interests of the United States by imposing new rules on the remittance of profits to the United States, expanding nationalization of American firms, and limiting natural resource concessions to foreigners. Regarding Cuba, the impact of the 1962 Cuban Missile Crisis led the Brazilian Foreign Ministry to review its position, particularly regarding the expulsion of Cuba from the Inter-American System.

In March 1964 a military coup changed the course of Brazilian political history. Though motivated by internal political developments, it occurred with the veiled blessing of the U.S. government. During the first phase of the military regime (1964–74), Brazil reverted to a policy of alignment with the United States and abandoned its autonomous foreign policy premises. Convergence with Western values under U.S. leadership again defined the ideological profile of Brazilian diplomacy, as the government of Castelo Branco (1964–67) agreed with the United States on the military and economic questions. Brazilian support for the Inter-American System was reinforced, especially through the newly created Inter-American Peace Force. The repeated adage of foreign minister Juracy Malgalhães (1966–67), that "whatever is good for the United States is also good for Brazil," became the new emblem for Brazilian foreign policy. Hence, Brazil broke relations with Cuba, participated in the invasion of the Dominican Republic (1965), and considered sending troops to Vietnam. Ideological and military affinity with the United States also reverberated in the economic realm, and new measures promoted the rapid elimination of the nationalistic policies that had hurt U.S. interests in Brazil.

In 1967, economic issues began to take a prominent position in the Brazilian diplomatic agenda. Under foreign minister Magalhães Pinto (1967–69), Brazilian foreign policy, based on a "diplomacy of prosperity," gave a new priority to the field of economic diplomacy. This tendency deepened as Brazilian economic policies again sought to promote national development.

Autonomy

The third phase in U.S.-Brazil relations began in 1974, during the second half of military rule in Brazil. Brazilian foreign policy went through major changes in the mid-1970s, based on the assumption that foreign affairs should meet national interests and become a crucial tool for economic development. Foreign economic policy was primarily motivated by the impact of the 1973 oil crisis and by new Brazilian industrial needs. It was now considered that while the diversification of trade, as well as foreign investors and financial sources, would strengthen the economy, an autonomous foreign policy would open doors for Brazil's interests abroad. Autonomy in foreign affairs would involve a nonideological foreign policy (i.e., disconnecting from the Cold War agenda), close ties with the third world, and ending the constraints posed by the alignment with the United States. Beginning in 1974, during the administration of Ernesto Geisel (1974–78), Brazil transformed its foreign policy to one grounded in autonomy, pragmatism and universalism.

Accordingly, Brazil pursued critical changes in its relations with the United States. At first, this implied upgrading the relationship with the United States, and Brazil's foreign minister Francisco Azevedo da Silveira (1974–78) sought to establish a new level of understanding with Washington by substituting traditional alignment with a new "special relationship." Thus, Silveira and U.S. secretary of state Henry Kissinger signed a Memorandum of Understanding in 1976, which was intended to provide for reciprocal consultation on common interests, and semiannual meetings, through which Brazil hoped to achieve a more symmetrical relationship with the United States.

However, this initiative fizzled shortly after the administration of Jimmy Carter came to office in the United States (1977–81). The Carter administration's concerns for human rights and nuclear proliferation would affect relations with most of the military regimes in Latin America, including that of Brazil. The Carter administration vehemently wanted to circumscribe Brazil's nuclear program, which was based upon cooperation with Germany. Such stringent U.S. pressures, however, produced an anti-U.S. reaction within Brazil's military as well as its diplomatic, political, and scientific circles. In 1977 Brazil denounced the 1952 military agreement with the United States and continued its nuclear projects with Germany. For the Geisel administration the nuclear program had become a symbol of autonomous development and security sovereignty.

After a period of high tension, U.S.-Brazil relations entered a low-profile phase that remained until the end of the Brazilian military regime. This political distance was accompanied by a more complex economic agenda, marked by the participation of U.S. financial entities in the growing Brazilian external debt, the increase in exports of manufactured and semimanufactured Brazilian products for the U.S. market, and the growing presence of U.S. investment in Brazil. For the next fifteen years, misunderstandings involving trade, finance, technology, security, and environmental matters expanded in U.S.-Brazil relations.

During the administration of João Figueiredo (1979–85), the tone in U.S.-Brazil relations was one of reciprocal disdain. Even though Brazil condemned the 1979 Soviet invasion of Afghanistan, it refused to adhere to sanctions proposed by the United Nations and the United States. And as expectations for a rapprochement—stimulated by President Ronald Reagan's 1982 visit to Brazil—failed, disagreements arose in different areas.

Brazilian diplomats observed U.S. actions in Central America with concern. They also deplored the U.S. intervention in Grenada (1983), and opposed the creation of a proposed South Atlantic Treaty Organization that would include the participation of Argentina and South Africa. This lack of understanding also affected military cooperation, as the U.S. government opposed Brazil's sensitive technology programs in the fields of microelectronics, aerospace materials, and long-range missiles.

In the meantime, the U.S.-Brazil trade agenda also found new complexities. Apart from the problems created by the use of protectionist measures that affected its exports, Brazil became a target for U.S. coercive diplomacy practices. These economic pressures intensified, first due to the Brazilian export incentive programs, and later due to its market reserve policy, particularly in the information technology sector. Furthermore, new differences between the two countries emerged over the new General Agreement on Tariffs and Trade agenda. Brazil opposed the inclusion of new issues—services and intellectual property—in multilateral negotiations and soundly resisted United States pressure in favor of unilateral economic liberalization.

In 1985, Brazil initiated its transition to democracy with the inauguration of the administration of José Sarney (1985–90). Again, the U.S. government did not welcome Brazil's foreign policy postures during the initial phase of democratization. At this time, Brazil took a critical view of U.S. military involvement in Central America, voiced its frustration over the lack of political attention toward the Latin American debt crisis, and became increasingly upset over coercive U.S. trade practices. New trade controversies blossomed after the U.S. Trade Representative initiated a series of investigations against Brazil under Section 301.[7] The U.S. decision evolved from lawsuits aimed at numerous countries accused of commercial malpractice. Disputes over computer hardware and software also increased.

At this time, military submission to the civil authorities in Brazil was reduced under the new 1988 constitution: the formal presence of military authorities in the government continued, and they held an implicit veto power in all topics related to international security. With respect to foreign policy matters, innovations were carefully negotiated between the Foreign Ministry and the military authorities. In the newly created Science and Technology Ministry, concerns shared by the military and the scientific community regarding technological autonomy were vigorously pursued. Simultaneously, the Brazilian military became more concerned with its presence in the Amazon region, an area of growing attention in the United States as a result of the expansion of environmental movements and organizations.

ADJUSTMENT

In 1990, a new set of domestic and international factors, including the end of the Cold War and economic globalization, along with democratic consolidation and economic reforms in Brazil, led to a process of gradual change in U.S.-Brazil relations. As the United States reviewed its Latin American policy, Brazil slowly abandoned its defensive posture vis-à-vis the United States.

Adjustments in international security policies, together with the implementation of an ample set of liberal economic policies, contributed to the rebuilding of bridges between the two countries. As Brazilian democratization began to consolidate, the government advanced major changes in foreign policy. These were aimed at stimulating closer relations with industrialized countries and would leave behind Brazil's previous autonomous stances in world affairs, most of which had become a source of friction with the United States.

Motivated by the need to deepen Brazil's international competitiveness and to improve the countries' access to markets, credit, and technology, the administration of Fernando Collor de Mello (1990–92) reshaped the country's foreign policy premises. The environment, human rights, and nonproliferation were no longer addressed with defensive postures, and international pressures were more accepted. In the economic realm, the government announced a series of new reforms, leading to economic openness, investment liberalization, privatization of state enterprises, and the renegotiation of the external debt. In regional affairs, the most important step was the formation, together with Argentina, Paraguay, and Uruguay, of MERCOSUR (Mercado Comun del Cono Sur, or Southern Cone Common Market), with the aim of deepening the commitment to open regionalism.

Nevertheless, prospects for a more cooperative relationship with the United States suffered a setback with the 1991 Persian Gulf War. Though the Brazilian government condemned the Iraqi government and favored the United Nations Security Council's decision to apply economic sanctions against the aggressor, it did not endorse military action against Iraq, as the United States had hoped.

Domestically, Brazilian reality soon revealed how fragile the domestic grounds were for enforcing the changes that had been announced by the new government. The resistance on the part of the political and economic elites to neoliberal reforms, together with a general rejection of the abuses of power by the new president and his closest collaborators, led to Collor de Mello's impeachment. As Vice President Itamar Franco assumed the presidency, Brazil faced a dramatic crisis of governability dominated by general macroeconomic disorder, in which the Brazilian Congress became a major source of stability and democratic continuity. Significantly, even as Brazil faced a serious and unpredictable domestic crisis, the military kept its distance from domestic politics and defended democratic order.

Franco took on the presidency in October 1992, and foreign policy during his administration (1992–94) emphasized Brazil's multifaceted international identities: a continental nation, a global player, and a relevant actor in hemispheric affairs. The prominent issues on Brazil's diplomatic agenda included the expansion of MERCOSUR, the formation of a South American Free Trade Area, the depoliticizing of relations with the United States, and rapprochement with such major powers as China, India, and Russia.

After Brazil's monthly inflation rate reached a peak of 40 percent, the Real Plan was launched in March 1994. The plan was Brazil's sixth attempt to achieve economic stabilization, this time under the conduct of finance minister Fernando Henrique Cardoso. The plan succeeded, and the country rapidly recovered international credibility. Furthermore, the success of the Real Plan would pave the way for Cardoso's victory in the 1994 presidential elections.

Brazil's international affairs during the Cardoso government (1995–2002) rested on four pillars: the essential foreign-policy premises, economic stability, democratic consolidation, and presidential diplomacy. In the international security realm, Brazil increased its commitment to nonproliferation regimes: it renounced any intention of producing, acquiring, or transferring long-range missiles, signed the Treaty on Conventional Weapons, and adhered to the Missile Technology Control Regime. In 1997, Brazil also signed the Anti–Land Mine Treaty and, the following year, the Nuclear Non-Proliferation Treaty. All of these initiatives helped improve the tenor of U.S.-Brazil relations regarding international security.

Meanwhile, the approval of an intellectual property law by the Brazilian congress in 1996 ended the most serious trade dispute between the two countries, and a 1997 visit to Brazil by U.S. president Bill Clinton eased differences regarding the creation of a hemispheric free trade zone. In 1998, at the Santiago Summit, Brazil committed to assuming the copresidency, with the United States, of the Free Trade Agreement of the Americas. A few months later, Cardoso repaid Clinton's visit, further reinforcing the positive aspects of the agenda with the United States.

Brazilian diplomacy since 1995 has tried to combine its interests and concerns in the world order with a positive relationship with the United States. The complexities and results of these efforts will be addressed in the following sections of this book.

CHRONOLOGY OF MAJOR EVENTS IN U.S.-BRAZIL RELATIONS

1824
May: The United States becomes the first nation to recognize Brazilian independence.

1827
March: U.S.-Brazil relations are temporarily suspended, due to U.S. opposition to Brazil's blockade in the River Plate Basin.

1828
December: Brazil signs the Navigation and Trade Treaty with the United States.

1889
October: Brazil participates in the first Inter-American Conference (hosted in Washington, D.C.), which leads to the creation of the Bureau of American Republics.
November: Argentina, the United States, and Uruguay recognize Brazil's new republican regime.

1891
January: Brazil signs a commercial treaty with the United States guaranteeing the free entry of Brazilian coffee into the United States in exchange for a 25 percent Brazilian tariff reduction on U.S. products.

1893
September: A naval rebellion begins in Brazil, during which the United States together with Great Britain, France, and Portugal act as mediators.

1894
August: The United States denounces the 1891 commercial treaty with Brazil.

1898
November: Brazil announces its neutrality in the Spanish-American War.

1905
January: Brazil inaugurates its first embassy abroad in Washington, D.C. In reciprocation, the United States establishes an embassy in Rio de Janeiro, the first in South America.

1909

January: Brazil signs a treaty of arbitration with the United States.

1913

June: Lauro Muller is the first Brazilian foreign minister to visit the United States.

1914

May: Argentina, Brazil, and Chile mediate the U.S.-Mexico dispute resulting from the U.S. occupation of the Mexican city of Veracruz.

1919

November: Brazil participates in the first International Labor Organization Conference in Washington.

1920

December: U.S. secretary of state Bainbridge Colby visits Brazil.

1923

October: Brazil signs a commercial modus vivendi with the United States, containing the inclusion of Most Favored Nation status.

1928

December: U.S. president-elect Herbert Hoover visits Brazil.

1930

November: Argentina, Cuba, Great Britain, Paraguay and the United States, among others, recognize Brazil's provisional government.

1935

February: Brazil signs a new commercial treaty with the United States.

1936

December: U.S. undersecretary of state Sumner Welles visits Brazil.

1937

June–July: An economic mission led by Brazilian minister of economy Souza Costa visits the United States.

1939

February–March: A mission led by Brazilian foreign minister Oswaldo Aranha visits the United States to discuss U.S.-Brazil relations. Brazil signs an economic agreement with the United States providing for U.S. aid for the formation of the Brazilian Central Bank.

June: The chief of the Brazilian army, Goes Monteiro, visits the United States.

1940

September: Brazil signs an agreement with the United States negotiating the financing of a steel plant in Volta Redonda.

1941

January: Brazil signs an agreement with the United States allowing for a U.S. military mission in Brazil.

October: Brazil and the United States agree that weapons will be provided to Brazil under the Lend-Lease Program.

1942

January: The third Consultation Reunion, with the presence of Latin American and U.S. foreign ministers, takes place in Rio de Janeiro. Brazil, along with other countries, agrees to break relations with the Axis powers.

February: A mission led by Brazilian minister of economy Souza Costa visits the United States to negotiate the provision of war materials to Brazil.

March: Brazil allows U.S. troops to be stationed on Brazilian soil. Brazil and the United States sign the Washington Agreement in which the United States agress to lend $100 million to finance a steel plant in Brazil, and to a $200 million credit for reequipping the Brazilian armed forces.

1943

January: U.S. president Franklin D. Roosevelt meets with Brazilian president Getúlio Vargas at the Natal aerial base.

August: War minister General Eurico Gaspar Dutra visits the United States to discuss the shipment of arms for the Brazilian army.

1944

June: Brazil signs an agreement for military aviation cooperation with the United States.

1945

February: U.S. secretary of state Edward Stettinius visits Brazil.

1946

August: U.S. general Dwight D. Eisenhower visits Brazil.

1947

August: U.S. president Harry Truman visits Brazil, and the United States and Brazil, together with other Latin American nations, sign the Inter-American Treaty for Reciprocal Assistance in Rio de Janeiro.

1948

April: Brazil signs the charter of the Organization of American States (OAS) in Bogotá, Colombia.

1949

May: Brazilian president Eurico Dutra visits the United States.

1950

December: A joint U.S.-Brazil commission on economic development is created.

1951

December: Brazil negotiates the supply of manganese, uranium, and monazite sand to the United States.

1952

March: Brazil and the United States sign a military assistance treaty.
July: U.S. secretary of state Dean Acheson visits Brazil.

1955

August: Brazil and the United States sign a cooperative agreement regulating the use of atomic energy.

1957

January: Brazil signs an agreement permitting the United States to install a missile-watch base on the island of Fernando de Noronha.

1958

August: U.S. secretary of state John Foster Dulles visits Brazil.

1960

February: U.S. president Dwight D. Eisenhower visits Brazil.
April: Brazilian president João Goulart visits the United States.

1962

December: U.S. attorney general Robert F. Kennedy visits Brazil to discuss indemnities for U.S. firms in the Brazilian region of Rio Grande do Sul.

1963

March: Brazilian minister of agriculture San Tiago Dantas visits the United States.

1965

April: Brazil joins the Inter-American Peace Force in the Dominican Republic under the command of Brazilian general Hugo Panasco Alvim.

1967

February: Brazilian president general Arthur da Costa e Silva visits the United States.

1971

December: Brazilian president General Garrastazu Medici visits the United States.

1972

September: Brazil and the United States sign an agreement to construct a nuclear power plant in Angra dos Reis.

1976

February: Brazil and the United States sign a Memorandum of Understanding.

1977

February: U.S. undersecretary of state Warren Christopher visits Brazil to discuss U.S. policy on nuclear nonproliferation.
March: The 1952 U.S.-Brazil military agreement is denounced.

1982

May: Brazilian president João Batista Figueiredo visits the United States.
December: U.S. president Ronald Reagan visits Brazil.

1983

October: Brazil announces its opposition to U.S. intervention in Grenada.

1984

February: U.S. secretary of state George Schultz visits Brazil and signs a military-industrial cooperation agreement between Brazil and the United States.

1986

September: Brazilian president José Sarney visits the United States.

1990

September: Brazilian president Fernando Collor de Melo visits the United States.

December: U.S. president George H. W. Bush visits Brazil.

1994

December: Brazil participates in the first Summit of the Americas in Miami, Florida.

1995

April: Brazilian president Fernando Henrique Cardoso visits the United States.

1997

October: U.S. president Bill Clinton visits Brazil.

1998

April: Brazil participates in the Second Summit of the Americas in Santiago de Chile.

June: Cardoso visits the United States and announces the creation of the National Antidrug Secretariat.

1999

May: Cardoso visits the United States.

2000

March: Brazilian foreign minister Luiz Felipe Lampreia visits the United States to meet secretary of state Madeleine Albright, secretary of commerce William Dale, and trade representative Charlene Barschefsky in order to review U.S.-Brazil relations.

2001

March: Cardoso visits the United States to deepen bilateral relations and regional affairs.

April: Brazil participates in the Third Summit of the Americas in Quebec.

September: Brazil participates in an extraordinary session of the Permanent Council of the OAS, together with all its members, in support of the United States after the terrorist attacks of September 11.

2002

April: Brazilian foreign minister Celso Lafer meets with U.S. trade representative Robert Zoellick in the United States to discuss bilateral and regional trade matters.

August: Brazil and the United States sign a Memorandum of Understanding for preventive action against narcotrafficking.

November: The seventh Free Trade Agreement of the Americas ministerial takes place in Quito, Ecuador; Brazil and the United States agree to cochair the negotiations until 2005.

December: Brazilan president-elect Luiz Inácio Lula da Silva visits the United States for his first meeting with President George W. Bush.

CHAPTER 2

New Complexities in U.S.-Brazil Economic Relations

The General Frame

Since the mid-1970s, u.s.-brazil economic relations have evolved against a continuously tense background. Because of its debt crisis and new global financial circumstances, Brazil became more exposed to international economic pressures. Hence, due to increases in both its asymmetrical interdependence and its external economic vulnerability, Brazil has lost bargaining power vis-à-vis the United States and has become subordinated to a more complex set of interests and pressures.

Meanwhile, the democratization process in Brazil has generated new trends in domestic politics in which a variety of political and economic interests exert their influence on internal and external affairs. Democratic consolidation has constrained the relative autonomy of the executive power, as business segments, political parties, and even trade unions have expanded their influence, especially in congressional politics. The Foreign Ministry remains the main state agency in charge of bilateral, regional, and multilateral trade negotiations dealing with a variety of domestic pressures, but it shares growing responsibilities with other agencies, especially the Ministries of Development and Agriculture, while monetary and financial external matters are handled by the Ministry of the Economy. In the United States, economic relations with Latin America countries are a result of three government agencies: the Department of the Treasury, which handles financial and monetary affairs, and the Department of Commerce and the U.S. Trade Representative, which together handle bilateral and regional trade matters.

Ever since the administration of Fernando Collor de Mello (1990–92), U.S. business and government circles have expected that Brazilian economic policies would adjust to mainstream liberal recipes. These expectations were stimulated by the renewed scenario in Latin America dominated by promising experiences of economic liberalization and stabilization. But political uncertainties between

Collor's impeachment in September 1992 and Fernando Henrique Cardoso's in-auguration in 1995 delayed these changes. Since then Brazil has moderated its adherence to free-market economics; it has moved ahead in liberalizing its econ-omy but has not given up its industrial development strategies.

Economic relations between Brazil and the United States face new challenges that involve four different dimensions. Furthermore, the way in which these di-mensions interplay with governmental and private interests has become critical, both for the enhancement of common interests and for the upsurge of controver-sies and misperceptions in bilateral relations.

The first dimension pertains to the evolution of Brazilian economics, the ex-pectations raised in the United States, and their impact on U.S. direct investment in Brazil. Over the past twenty-five years, the results of structural adjustment policies have influenced the perceptions and expectations in the U.S. business community, the U.S. government, and Washington-based international financial institutions the International Monetary Fund (IMF) and the World Bank. Brazil's only gradual adherence to liberal economic policies has been a constant source of criticism within the United States, and officials constantly voice their disappoint-ment with Brazil in blunt terms. Statements have been made calling for more transparency in privatization, for market liberalization, and especially for the en-forcement of an effective fiscal reform. In this last case, Brazil is criticized for its heavy taxation system, which consumes close to 30 percent of its gross domestic product.[1]

In the last ten years, as Brazil has become exposed to global financial turmoil and speculative monetary attacks, the country struggled to conserve room for maneuvering when handling critical situations. Nevertheless, the continuity of Brazil's economic stability has involved recurrent monitoring and endorsement from the IMF and World Bank. The most critical situation took place in early 1999, when the country faced a dramatic currency crisis.

A second and more traditional dimension relates to commercial transactions between both countries. This has been an important aspect of bilateral relations all through the twentieth century. Contrary to what had been expected, trade lib-eralization measures in Brazil did not contribute to the overcoming of bilateral discrepancies. Brazil resents the lack of reciprocity on the part of U.S. policies, while the United States has pressured Brazil to deepen its open-market polices in the belief that Brazil should openly face the lack of competitiveness of its indus-tries. These bilateral trade discrepancies gradually spilled over into the arena of multilateral trade negotiations.

A third dimension has gained importance in recent years, as multilateral institutionalism became even more important in world trade. Since the creation of the World Trade Organization (WTO) in 1992, U.S.-Brazil trade disputes have gained a new visibility in the multilateral fora. These disputes have been solved in the WTO in compliance with the set of rules and regulations that both countries have agreed to follow.

The fourth dimension also goes beyond strictly bilateral ties, and engages the most recent facet of U.S.-Brazil economic relations involving a regional dimension. Since the launching of the North American Free Trade Agreement (NAFTA) on the one hand and the Mercado Comun del Cono Sur (Common Market of the Southern Cone, or MERCOSUR) on the other, a new agenda has emerged between both countries. Both the United States and Brazil are the leading markets in their subregional economic integration arrangements, and as a consequence they are both the major players in the Free Trade Agreement for the Americas (FTAA) negotiations. MERCOSUR-U.S. negotiations became a decisive factor in the ongoing FTAA negotiations, which are to be concluded in 2005. Nevertheless, as FTAA negotiations progress it has become clear that Brazil's resistance goes beyond the MERCOSUR frame. Increasingly, Brazil has assumed an individual stance toward the creation of a hemispheric free trade area transposing to these negotiations the same complaints and demands placed in bilateral terms.

These four dimensions will now be addressed in greater detail in the following sections.

DOMESTIC ECONOMICS AND U.S. DIRECT INVESTMENT

After almost ten years of frustrating attempts, Brazil's mid-1994 stabilization program promised enduring and positive results. In July 1994, the introduction of a new currency, the *real*, led to a decline in inflation, from an average monthly rate over 40 percent to less than 2 percent. While this restored domestic and international confidence,[2] Brazil's tight monetary policies and very high interest rates constrained the expansion of its economy.

Based on a strongly valued currency and high interest rates, these new economic policies made Brazil attractive to foreign capital. Trade liberalization, already undertaken in the early 1990s under the new currency, stimulated a rapid expansion of Brazilian imports. Meanwhile, privatization gradually advanced, opening key economic areas to foreign investment.

Brazilian economic policies improved the domestic environment for private transnational capital. Whereas the Real Plan changed the country's international image, U.S. business and governmental circles welcomed Brazil's more open and competitive economy, and improvements in economic performance became an important incentive for the augmentation and diversification of foreign investment. Measures facilitating investments from abroad in the financial, telecommunications, and transportation sectors led to a major expansion in flows coming from different OECD countries. Besides the role played by Brazil's attractive economic scenario, U.S. investment was also stimulated by the economic growth at home.

TABLE 2.1

Global U.S. Foreign Direct Investment, 1998

Rank	Country	Amount (US $ millions)
1	United Kingdom	178,648
2	Canada	103,908
3	Netherlands	79,386
4	Germany	42,853
5	France	39,188
6	Japan	38,153
7	Brazil	37,802
8	Switzerland	37,616
9	Australia	33,676
10	Panama	26,957
11	Mexico	25,877
12	Hong Kong	20, 802

Note: Bermuda has been excluded from this list as a special case representing mainly financial investment (91 percent of the $41 billion country total). Had Bermuda been included, it would have ranked fifth and Brazil eighth.
Source: http://www.ambaixada-americana.org.br/usfdi99.htm

Between 1991 and 1998, the United States, the long-standing major source of foreign investment in Brazil, more than tripled its investment in the country, so that by 1998 U.S. foreign direct investment (USFDI) in Brazil approached $38 billion, concentrating mostly in the financial and manufacturing sectors (chemical, transportation, and food; see Tables 2.2 and 2.3). Telecommunications and transportation were the biggest growth sectors of USFDI in Brazil as a result of

TABLE 2.2

Composition and Growth of USFDI: Composition and Growth Rates of Brazil's Manufacturing Sector, 1994 and 1998

Subsector	Share 1994 (%)	Share 1998 (%)
Food	12	11
Chemicals	18	25
Metals	7	6
Machinery	8	7
Electronics	9	9
Transportation	17	15
Others	30	27
Total	100	100

Source: http://www.embaixada-americana.org.br/usfdi99.htm

TABLE 2.3

U.S. Direct Investment Profile, 1998 (Percentage Shares)

Sector	World	South America	South America (Brazil excluded)	Brazil only
Petroleum	9	10	14	5
Manufacturing	31	41	23	59
Wholesale Trade	8	3	4	1
Banking	4	6	9	4
Finance	35	16	19	13
Services	5	4	4	4
Others	8	20	27	14

Source: http://www.embaixada-americana.org.br/usfdi99.htm

the participation of U.S. firms in privatization and concessions sales. Brazil became the sixth leading country in total USFDI, and the first in the third world, counting for over 50 percent of U.S. overseas investment in South America (see Tables 2.1, 2.2, and 2.3).

Notwithstanding all the changes produced by privatization, the process is considered incomplete by U.S. officials who complain that crucial areas such as the petroleum and the electrical energy sectors were left out. In addition, other complaints and expectations soon surfaced involving tax administration, customs procedures, enforcement of intellectual property rights, and increased transparency in economic regulations.

The expansion of U.S. direct investment in Brazil coincided with an important increase of the presence of other countries, especially Spain (see Table 2.4). In fact, as the figures below show, by the year 2000 Spanish investment in Brazil surpassed that of the United States.

Brazil's investment has increased in the United States as well, and an important group of Brazilian firms have managed to expand their presence there. This

TABLE 2.4

Foreign Direct Investment in Brazil, 1999–2000

Country	1999	2000
Spain	20.0%	21.3%
USA	29.4%	20.6%
Portugal	—	10.6%
France	7.0%	8.2%
Netherlands	7.2%	7.2%

Source: Central Bank of Brazil

includes firms such as Amil (health insurance); Citrosuco and Cutrale (juice processors); Vale do Rio Doce (mining); Embraer (aircraft); Gerdau (steel); Ipope (polls); Odebrecht (construction and petrochemicals); Petrobras (oil); and Embraco, Romi, and Ioschpe (machinery and mechanics).

In the next few years U.S. direct investment in Brazil will tend to decrease as a consequence of three unrelated factors: the slowdown in U.S. economic growth, the end of relevant privatization processes in Brazil, and the new vulnerabilities of the Brazilian economy after its 1999 monetary crisis.

Due to the effects of the Russian devaluation and debt default of August 1998, Brazil suffered a speculative attack on its currency that reduced its foreign reserves by $30 billion in five months. At the time, the Brazilian government managed to obtain crucial external support, particularly from the United States, to help it weather the changes it made in its monetary policy.[3] A rescue package of $41.5 billion set up by the IMF was followed by the adoption of a new exchange rate regime that led to a dramatic depreciation of the local currency.[4] The growth rate of the Brazilian economy fell while the dramatic inflationary impact of devaluation was somewhat avoided thanks to thorough monetary measures, of which high interest rates became an inevitable part.

Under these circumstances, Brazil's public debt increased dramatically during the late 1990s. A reasonable situation in which the public debt represented less than 30 percent of the gross domestic product was replaced by an alarming scenario in which it surpassed 60 percent. By the end of the Cardoso administration the repetition of financial speculative waves had slowed economic growth and kept debt payment extremely high. Though foreign investment did not reach the high standards of the mid-1990s, it did not fall, as had been expected. In fact, in 2000 foreign direct investment in Brazil reached $33.5 billion dollars.

These fragile economic conditions persisted until the presidential elections of October 2002. New monetary speculative waves also took place, stimulated by the deep economic and political crisis in Argentina and then by the electoral uncertainties in Brazil. However, the markets and investors gradually calmed with the approval of a $30 billion IMF loan granted after a political negotiation led by the Cardoso administration was accepted by all presidential candidates at the time. Later, the initial external concerns caused by the victory of the left-wing Workers' Party leader Luiz Inácio Lula da Silva were lessened, as the newly elected president promised that the financial commitments assumed by the previous government would be honored.

U.S.-BRAZIL TRADE: A RENEWED AGENDA

U.S.-Brazil trade relations reflected new complexities throughout the 1990s. Two-way trade increased from $12 billion in 1990 to $19 billion in 1995, and to $23 billion in 1999. And although Brazil maintained a trade surplus with the

United States throughout the 1980s, the situation now changed: U.S. exports to Brazil increased dramatically in number and relative importance, but Brazilian exports to the United States hardly expanded at all. By the mid-1990s, Brazil showed a continuous deficit with the United States (see Table 2.5). It should also be noted that this picture was part of a general trend in Brazil's trade balance.

In 1994 and 1995, after the Real Plan was launched, the United States accounted for approximately 50 percent of Brazil's total trade deficit. This tendency was first associated with Brazil's new currency, and later with the slowdown of economic growth rates.[5] After 1999, expectations that U.S.-Brazil trade would become more balanced increased as a result of two new factors: the impact of the devaluation of Brazil's currency since early 1999 and the growing importance of intracompany trade in bilateral transactions. But while the trade imbalance became less dramatic, it did not cease. In 1999 the surplus with Brazil represented 60 percent of

TABLE 2.5

Brazil's Trade with the United States (US$)

Year	Exports	Percentage of Total Exports	Imports	Percentage of Total Imports
1980	3,439,945,327	17.09	4,071,064,954	17.73
1981	4,040,209,811	17.35	3,480,726,882	15.75
1982	3,980,314,269	19.73	2,837,057,840	14.63
1983	4,989,723,885	22.78	2,381,539,073	15.44
1984	7,603,105,766	28.15	2,254,142,052	16.20
1985	6,844,516,090	26.70	2,589.906,819	19.69
1986	6,174,414,512	27.63	3,186,732,800	22.89
1987	7,191,843,782	27.42	3,145,159,833	20.90
1988	8,835,721,197	26.15	3,086,836,475	21.13
1989	8,231,202,141	23.94	3,870,852,482	21.19
1990	7,594,263,027	24.17	4,392,958,502	21.26
1991	6,264,436,712	19.81	4,938,211,089	23.47
1992	6,932,757,328	19.37	4,538,666,763	22.08
1993	7,843,335,397	20.34	5,062,251,046	20.04
1994	8,816,241,304	20.25	6,674,390,616	20.18
1995	8,628,812,181	18.67	10,519,498,419	21.05
1996	9,182,584,604	19.23	11,718,968,898	21.99
1997	9,276,013,005	17.51	14,138,597,527	23.05
1998	9,740,882,641	19.05	13,337,589,980	23.25
1999	10,849,000,000	22.60	11,727,000,000	23.8
2000	13,180,528,710	23.93	12,894,269,157	23.09
2001	14,189,601,558	24.37	12,893,626,797	23.20

Source: Ministerio do Desenvolvimento, Industria e Comercio, *Intercambio Comercial Brasileiro Estados Unidos* (1980–2001 figures), http://www.mdic.gov.br/indicadores/intercambio.htm

TABLE 2.6

Brazil's Participation in U.S. Imports (US$ Millions)

| | U.S. Imports | | Percentage of |
	Brazil	Total	Brazilian Participation
1990	8.585	517.524	1.7
1991	7.222	508.944	1.4
1992	8.144	553.496	1.5
1993	8.021	603.153	1.3
1994	9.307	689.030	1.3
1995	9.296	770.821	1.2
1996	10.149	817.627	1.1
1997	10.642	898.025	1.1
1998	10.784	944.350	1.1

Source: BADECEL-CEPAL

the U.S. surplus in all the Americas, and out of all its other trading partners, the United States enjoyed its fourth largest trade surplus with Brazil.

As U.S. surplus trade with Brazil became constant, the importance of the Brazilian market increased for U.S. exports. In 1997 and 1988 Brazil became the eleventh largest export market for the United States. Though Brazilian exports to the United States did not decrease during the 1990s, U.S. exports to Brazil doubled between 1994 and 2000. But even this has not stopped U.S. complaints regarding Brazilian trade barriers that affected U.S. goods and services.

As mentioned earlier, the changing patterns of U.S.-Brazil trade became part of a new scenario of Brazil's mounting trade deficits generated mainly by the strengthening of its currency. Hence, the expansion of U.S. exports to Brazil was more a consequence of trade liberalization than of economic growth. U.S. exports to Brazil have been dominated by capital goods and high-tech industrial inputs, most of which is in intracompany trade, resulting from the growing presence of U.S. multinationals in Brazil (see Table 2.7).[6]

After the 1999 devaluation, it was widely expected that Brazil would improve its trade balance, as exports expanded to the country's main trading partners, and in fact Brazil was able to decrease significantly its bilateral trade deficit with the United States. By the end of 2000 its commercial ties had reached an equilibrium not seen since the early 1990s, and this revealed an important expansion of Brazilian exports to the United States. Furthermore, while Brazil's exports to the United States were 18–19 percent of its total exports in the period 1995–98, they rose to 22–23 percent in the years 1999–2001. Brazilian officials were quite emphatic that this growth was a consequence of greater competitiveness, not the result of any sort of reduction in U.S. trade barriers.

TABLE 2.7

Brazil's Top Ten Imports from the United States, January–September 2000

Item	Import Value (US$ Millions)
Telecommunications equipment	553
Computers and Microchips	692
Aircraft Engines	356
Electrical Equipment	253
Medicine	245
Measuring Equipment	229
Chemicals	181
Telephone Equipment	180
Auto parts	158

Source: http://www.embaixada-americana.org.br/hitech.htm

U.S. trade policies have represented a continuous source of friction for Brazil. Though the United States has one of the lowest tariff systems in world trade—4.5 percent is the average—discriminatory measures have led to the application of an average tariff of 45.6 percent on the fifteen top Brazilian exports to the U.S. market. These fifteen products represent 36.4 percent of Brazilian total exports.[7] The average tariff imposed on the fifteen most important U.S. exports to Brazil does not surpass 14.3 percent.

Brazilian agricultural products represent only 0.2 percent of total U.S. agricultural imports (see Table 2.8). An interesting parallel can be made with Mexico, which now represents over 40 percent of U.S. agricultural imports.

The U.S. tariff rate quota system has affected Brazilian products such as sugar, which has been excluded from the General System Preference since 1989, and tobacco. As a consequence of U.S. quota policies, tariffs imposed upon Brazilian sugar were 236 percent, and 350 percent on tobacco.

TABLE 2.8

U.S. Imports of Fresh Fruits and Vegetables, 2000

Total World Imports	US$ 4.2 Billion	100%
Latin America	US$ 3.6 billion	85.7%
Mexico	US$ 1.7 billion	40.5%
South America	US$ 959 million	22.8%
Chile	US$ 402 million	9.6%
Brazil	US$ 8.6 million	0.2%

Source: http://www.embaixada-americana.org.br/comercio.htm

However, in some cases, Brazilian exporters have been able to adapt to U.S. trade restrictions. Such is the case with the exportation of Brazilian concentrated orange juice, which has been partially displaced by Mexican exports and U.S. production in Florida. At first, Brazilian orange juice exports to the United States were encouraged by American growers and processors because of the frequent frost devastation to Florida's citrus crops. After a spectacular penetration in the early 1980s, when Brazilian orange juice made up 45 percent of the American market, Florida growers managed to get the U.S. government to authorize the imposition of antidumping measures, which by 1998 had reduced this to 12 percent, allowing American growers to control 64 percent of the market. Tariffs on Brazilian juice can range as high as 63 percent. Among the strategies to counter the U.S. barriers, a group of Brazilian firms bought processing plants in Florida, which allowed them to influence prices for bulk juice purchased from either Florida or Brazil. By the mid-1990s, Brazilian companies managed to control 30 percent of the concentrated orange juice business in Florida.

Brazilian manufactured products have faced increasing difficulties penetrating the U.S. market. Brazilian footwear and textiles have been displaced by Chinese industry, and steel has been continuously affected by antidumping and countervailing regulations. As Table 2.9 indicates, aircraft have dominated Brazilian exports to the United States, followed by shoes and auto parts.

In recent years, steel has been the most conflictive chapter in U.S.-Brazil trade. Brazil steel producers had once expected preferential negotiations similar to those granted to Russia, but since 2000 the enforcement of new trade barriers

TABLE 2.9

Brazil's Top Ten Exports to the United States, January–September 2000

Item	Export Value (US$ Millions)
Aircraft	932
Shoes	662
Auto Parts	364
Coffee Beans	362
Iron and Steel	342
Automobile Engines	278
Radios	238
Wood Pulp	229
Nonmonetary gold	216
Pumps and Compressors	198

Source: http://www.embaixada-americana.org.br/hitech

affecting steel products has opened a new round of complaints on the part of the Brazilian authorities.[8] Even though punitive duties on inexpensive steel were conceived mainly to curtail Japanese exports, the U.S. government has refused to apply preferential treatment to Brazilian steel products.

In early 2000, the imposition of antidumping duties on steel imports—particularly hot-rolled steel—was blocked by the United States International Trade Commission (USITC); this was a victory for companies from Argentina, Brazil, Japan, Russia, South Africa, and Thailand.[9] Nevertheless, that did not stop the powerful U.S. steel industry and unions from making new attempts to control the entry of inexpensive steel products. After the terrorist attack against the U.S. on September 11, 2001, the industry stated the need to consider its future a matter of national security and called for stronger sanctions against foreign products.[10]

These difficulties in trade have been accompanied by a tension and misunderstanding in official circles that have become public every time escalation has replaced positive negotiations. Public declarations by both U.S. and Brazilian officials often reveal a dialogue of the deaf that involves government, business sectors, and the media. For instance, during the cold-rolled steel episode, the lack of flexibility on the side of U.S. commerce authorities led the Brazilian Foreign Ministry to declare that trade relations with the United States were facing their worst moment in the past thirty years. Meanwhile, the newly appointed U.S. ambassador in Brazil used the USITC decision as an example of fair competition, portraying the accusations against U.S. protectionism as more a matter of misperceptions than of concrete reality.

Brazilian officials share the perception that U.S.-Brazil trade disputes have reached the point of exhaustion in intergovernmental negotiations. As Brazil recognizes the limited results of bilateral understanding in the face of continuous U.S. unilateral actions, it has fostered the expansion of a pro-Brazilian constituency in the United States. The attempts to stimulate a Brazilian caucus to improve penetration in the media and to support interfirm connections have become growingly important for Brazilian diplomacy. Both sides also realize that the cluster of bilateral trade misunderstandings will have an impact on the negotiations regarding the Free Trade Area of the Americas.

The Multilateral Dimension

Brazil's trade liberalization measures coincided with major changes in the global environment. The new institutional frame that began in the mid-1990s with the creation of the WTO expanded Brazil's exposure to international regulations. The country's use of contingency measures increased, as did its participation in multilateral consultations and panel reviews. And while trade liberalization measures progressed, Brazil made use of new instruments to deal with trade balance problems.

Between 1948 and 1991, Brazil was involved in only thirteen General Agreement on Tariffs and Trade (GATT) dispute settlements, in ten of them as a complainant. Only once were complaints against Brazil made by the United States, while on six occasions Brazil made complaints against the United States (see Table 2.10).

Between 1992 and 1996, the trade dispute settlements involving Brazil rose to seventeen. Of these, the United States raised six, three of which were against Brazil. In addition, five of the total of eight complaints raised in this period against Brazil came from NAFTA countries.[11]

Brazil now began for the first time to make use of various provisional safeguard measures to balance the effects of its liberalization polices.[12] In mid-1996, eighty-two antidumping and countervailing actions were in force against Brazil, twenty of which had been taken by the United States. If NAFTA were considered as a bloc, this number increases to forty-two, or more than 50 percent of the total. While steel products became the main target of U.S. actions, sugar, tobacco, orange juice, and footwear exports were also affected. Furthermore, Brazil has continuously been listed as a "priority foreign country" under the U.S. Special 301 Provision.[13]

TABLE 2.10

Dispute Settlements Involving Brazil and the United States, 1948–91

Description of Case	Complaint Date	Referred to
Complaints made by the United States		
Brazilian restrictions on imports of certain agricultural and manufactured goods	October 1989	Recourse to Article XXIII.2
Complaints made by Brazil		
U.S. imports of nonbeverage ethyl alcohol from Brazil	May 1986	Article XXIII.1 consultations
U.S. tariff increases and import prohibitions on products from Brazil	November 1987	Article XXIII:1 consultations and request for good office by the director general
U.S. import restrictions on products from Brazil	November 1988	Panel—February 1989
U.S. measures under the Export Enhancement Program affecting soybean oil exports by Brazil	February 1990	Request for Consultations under Article XXIII:1
U.S. denial of most favored nation treatment of nonrubber footwear from Brazil	August 1990	Panel—January 1992

Source: GATT Trade Policy Review 1992, vol. 1, 274–75.

Besides its involvement in numerous trade disputes, Brazil has been an active player in the international community regarding the rules and institutional buildup of the multilateral trade system. This has been an area of concern for Brazilian foreign policy since the early days of the GATT. As mentioned in the previous chapter, the Brazilian government was a firm advocate for the creation of the World Trade Organization (WTO) in 1995 and has since then adhered to the group of countries that demand a new round of multilateral trade negotiations, called the Millenium Round.[14]

Brazil has now concentrated its attention on two main subjects in multilateral trade negotiations: ending the subsidization of agriculture, which is particularly aimed at the European Union, and the flexibility of demands regarding new issues on the agenda. While in the first instance Brazil and the United States have shared similar views, in the second they differ. Brazil basically perceives itself as a global trader in need of greater access to markets and assumes a defensive posture toward new trade restrictions. After the fiasco at the Third Ministerial WTO meeting in Seattle in 2000, where an agreement regarding the agenda for a new round of global trade negotiations was not achieved among member states, a new attempt was made at Doha in 2001. This time, consensus for a new round of global trade negotiations was finally reached.

A major question for Brazil at the Doha meeting concerned the debate on pharmaceutical licensing and public health programs. The 1995 WTO Agreement on Trade-Related Aspects of Intellectual Property Rights (TRIPS) had determined the enforcement of intellectual property rights, including pharmaceutical patents, to take effect by 2003. The generic production of antiretroviral drugs at low production prices has become a large industry in Brazil. While it receives important support from local health authorities, the enforcement of the TRIPS provisions would affect not only the production of these generic variants, but the costs involved in the treatment of acquired immune deficiency syndome (AIDS).

The use of nonlicensed pharmaceuticals in Brazilian anti-AIDS programs had already become a touchy issue in U.S.-Brazil understandings on intellectual property, and at Doha two coalitions were formed: one led by Brazil and India, followed by a broad group of less developed countries, and the other by Australia, Canada, Germany, New Zealand, Switzerland, and the United States. While the first block stood for the inclusion of a more flexible interpretation of the TRIPS provisions in the case of public health necessities, the other did not.[15] Thanks to a last-minute switch by the United States, the first group finally prevailed. One important reason for the closer position between the United States and Brazil on this matter is the public health emergencies faced in the United States in which government needs and the pharmaceutical patent rights held by powerful private interests have not always coincided. A parallel can be traced between Brazilian public health programs against AIDS and the measures taken by the U.S.

government in 2001 against anthrax. In both cases government health policies favored generic pharmaceuticals against the interests of the private pharmaceutical industry.

The start of a new round of global trade negotiations in the near future will bring up new agendas, and convergences and discrepancies between Brazil and the United States on multilateral trade arrangements and norms. This process will take place simultaneously with the negotiations for the proposed Hemispheric Free Trade Agreement, as both are scheduled to conclude in 2005. While the agendas at stake are quite similar, positions regarding specific issues can be quite different.

THE REGIONAL DIMENSION

Negotiations regarding the FTAA have gained enormous importance in U.S.-Brazil relations, as they are part of a broader process of redefining foreign trade arrangements in which regionalism has tended to assume a new role. In both cases, these negotiations depend upon domestic support provided by political parties, business sectors, and labor organizations. In the United States, the early stage of regional trade talks took place during the administration of George H. W. Bush (1989–93); they deepened during the two administrations of Bill Clinton (1993–2001) and continue during the present administration of George W. Bush. In Brazil, negotiations first took place during the government of Collor, continued with Franco, deepened with the Cardoso administrations, and will conclude during the Lula administration. While internal politics have always been a crucial aspect of foreign trade policies in the United States, domestic political involvement and pressure regarding trade negotiations in Brazil represent a very recent phenomenon linked to the consolidation of democracy. Never before have trade negotiations been so politicized within the Brazilian society—especially those regarding the FTAA.

U.S. interests in constructing an integrated zone with Canada and Mexico planted the seeds for a hemispheric free trade area at the same time that Argentina and Brazil were taking their first steps toward the formation of a common market. In June 1990, in a meeting in Buenos Aires, the two countries created a regime of gradual automatic trade liberalization that was scheduled to be completed in 1994. In March 1991, the Treaty of Asunción extended the same system to Paraguay and Uruguay, forecasting the creation of a common market in the Southern Cone, now known as MERCOSUR.

Since the idea of a hemispheric integration project first surfaced in the early 1990s, Brazil has developed three different positions. First, when the Bush Initiative, also known as the Initiative of the Americas, was launched in 1990, Brazil showed disdain regarding the formation of a Free Trade Area of the Americas. Four years later, at the Miami Summit (1994), Brazil assumed a defensive posture dominated by zero-sum calculations that seemed to indicate that MERCOSUR and FTAA would be mutually exclusive. The third position emerged during the preparations for the 1998 Santiago Summit, where the formal negotiations for FTAA were launched. Brazil then assumed an affirmative position supported by two different motivations: the strength of its presence in MERCOSUR, and the convergence between government and societal organizations that facilitated the articulation of a "national" position toward the FTAA.[16] The advancement of these three positions will be briefly discussed here.

For the United States, the Initiative of the Americas, launched in June 1990, represented the recognition that the region's economic needs were indeed congruent with the recipes for economic stabilization recommended by international financial institutions and U.S. authorities. The preoccupation with stimulating investments and interchanges in the Americas primarily became a rhetorical exercise, with more political impact than anything else. The simultaneity of the Initiative of the Americas and the formation of MERCOSUR created the illusion of a four-plus-one negotiating process (MERCOSUR plus the United States), but this hypothesis rapidly dissipated. For the United States, NAFTA had become the space par excellence of negotiating preferential commercial agreements with the other countries in the Americas.

Notwithstanding, instead of stimulating a cooperative movement in Latin America, the idea that post-NAFTA negotiations would take place had a fragmenting effect that impeded the consolidation of a harmonious hemispheric negotiation process. While Brazil appeared to be less interested in the NAFTA spillovers, other countries, such as Argentina and Chile, appeared quite anxious to share Mexico's destiny. In the case of MERCOSUR, this fragmentation affected the Argentina-Brazil negotiating process and helped fuel Chile's reluctance to adhere to the bloc.[17]

At the same time, Brazilian political and business circles criticized the advancement of NAFTA negotiations, and highlighted two problematic aspects. They thought NAFTA would cause a geo-economic fragmentation between northern and southern Latin America, and they criticized the inclusion of new issues—labor standards and the environment—in trade negotiations. Brazil had opposed the inclusion of both issues in the GATT multilateral trade negotiations, and feared that NAFTA could potentially become a new channel for pressure on Brazil.

The NAFTA negotiating process coincided with the first positive effects of MERCOSUR on Brazilian foreign trade. In 1991–93, the relative importance of Brazilian exports to the subregion rose from 7 percent to 14 percent; Argentina became Brazil's second most important trading partner, and exports within MERCOSUR jumped from $11.1 billion to $18.5 billion. Regional integration began to be seen within Brazil as an opportunity to enhance its international

economic profile, and the idea of a South American trading bloc that would inte-
grate MERCOSUR, the Andean Pact, and Chile surfaced. This project was named
the South American Free Trade Area (SAFTA) and the idea that it stood in opposition to the FTAA became widespread in Brazil.

During the preparations of the 1994 Miami Summit, U.S. authorities feared
that Brazil's reluctance toward a hemispheric trade area would pose difficulties.[18]
When it was announced that the negotiations would lead to a free trade area in
2005, overcoming these difficulties became a top priority. Furthermore, a sched-
ule for ministerial meetings was set up and the project became a prominent item
on the foreign policy agendas of the countries in the region. After the Miami
Summit, the Brazilian government assessed the costs of its exclusion, and concentrated its efforts on broadening the FTAA time frames. Besides containing
U.S. pressure, Brazil needed time to accommodate and harmonize all the liberalization commitments that were at stake.

The creation of the FTAA had become one of the main topics on the hemispheric expanded agenda. From a U.S. perspective, this process involved the
dissolution of other subregional integration regimes such as the Central
American Common Market, the Andean Pact, and MERCOSUR. The United
States also assumed that a Washington-led process would deepen U.S. commitment to regionalism. For the executive branch it became crucial to obtain
fast-track authorization from Congress to carry forward the negotiations.
However, Mexico's 1995 "Tequila crisis" slowed down the rhythm of hemispheric negotiations and disrupted the United States political capacity to
include other countries of the region in preferential trade schemes. Brazil consequently gave top priority to MERCOSUR as a space of regional cooperation
and integration.

The commitments to deepen the subregional integration process within
MERCOSUR created the expectation that a customs union would soon be consolidated. Brazil's trade profile was strongly influenced by the consequences of the
Real Plan on the balance of payments. The overvaluation of the Brazilian
currency, in addition to liberalization policies enforced in the 1990s, substantially
augmented the country's deficit with the majority of the countries in the
Americas and contributed to a tremendous increase in Brazilian imports (from
$20.7 billion in 1990 to $53.3 billion in 1996). Within MERCOSUR, Brazilian
trade deficits accumulated to $2.24 billion between 1995 and 1997.

From a political perspective, Brazil worried far more about its deficit with the
United States than its deficits with its neighbors. The increased access of Latin
American products to the Brazilian market came to be seen as a political asset
that helped to downplay the asymmetries between Brazil and its partners. The
trade imbalance with the United States, however, became a source of concern, as it
was dissociated from a wider frame of reciprocal negotiations.

Within the United States, the Mexican crisis provoked a debate over the costs and benefits of NAFTA that forced the Clinton administration to change its strategy toward regionalism in the Americas. From this time on, domestic conditions increasingly restricted the U.S. government's freedom to maneuver in international trade negotiations.[19] After four years of emitting ambiguous political signals to Latin American governments, the White House decided to postpone asking Congress for approval of the FTAA. Besides being conscious of domestic constraints to expand hemispheric trade relations, the Democratic administration preferred to prioritize other foreign economic agendas such as the expansion of its contributions to the IMF and trade talks with China.[20]

A new series of meetings in the preparatory phases of the FTAA process took place in September 1996, and Brazil's temporary presidency of the negotiations generated a sense of the country's responsibility in articulating Latin American positions.[21] At the Third Commerce Ministers' Conference in Belo Horizonte in May 1997, Brazil assumed an affirmative position in the negotiating process based on the principles negotiated with all thirty-four states involved in the process: consensus; the indivisible nature of the negotiating package ("single undertaking"); compatibility with WTO rules; the coexistence between FTAA and the existing subregional and bilateral agreements; the a priori nonexclusion of any sector that involved access to markets or the elimination of barriers; and the conclusion of negotiations by 2005, when enforcement would begin.

The Brazilian government also tried to give its participation in the FTAA negotiating process a political spin, and the demands of Brazilian business sectors and labor organizations became part of the FTAA negotiating process. In Brazil, the FTAA became a relevant subject for public discussion, and growing nationalistic consensus has built up, supported by business sectors, labor movements, and partisan and academic segments. In all cases there has been a growing concern regarding the asymmetrical economic effects of trade liberalization if the United States does not review unilateral protectionism. The long-lasting consequences of U.S.-Brazil commercial disputes, particularly those in which Brazilian exports have been hurt by U.S. nontariff barriers, have helped to sustain this consensus.

In this context, a proposal for agreements on the FTAA negotiating process was successfully constructed, based on three premises: the indissolubility of MERCOSUR, gradualism in the negotiating process, and balance between costs and benefits. Further negotiations were to take place in three stages: (1) "business facilitation," with the reduction of transaction costs for the economic agents and the inclusion of measures like certificates of origin, the simplification of merchandise transportation, and the recognition of sanitation certificates; (2) harmonization of norms, with the elimination of unjustified nontariff restrictions and the definition of a mechanism for resolving controversies inside the free trade area; (3) and the opening of markets and tariff dismantling.

Following the 1998 Santiago Summit, the negotiating process for the creation of the FTAA became more complex. An ambiguous situation had been created, since the progression of the negotiating agenda was not accompanied by most important U.S. political signaling, the approval of fast-track legislation by the U.S. Congress. Furthermore, the Clinton administration's growing difficulty in assuring approval by its own party served to counter the belief that the administration would give more economic substance to its Latin American policies.

The main issues at stake in the FTAA negotiation process came to be adhering to the agreement, a methodology for overseeing the agreement, distributing the costs and benefits between unequal partners, and linking the agreement with the macroeconomic conditions of the countries in the region. For Brazil, this last item became crucial in light of the need to adjust FTAA negotiations with the economic reforms implemented in the previous years—economic deregulation, reductions of substantial restrictions to foreign capital, economic openness, and an ample privatization program.

Brazil expected that the preparatory phases of FTAA would allow for the betterment of its trade relations with the United States. Hence, for Brazil, the issues of major importance in the negotiating process became the reciprocal liberalization of agricultural products; the elimination of subsidies for agricultural, metallurgical products, shoes, and textiles; and measures against disloyal commercial practices.

When it came to power in 2001 the Bush administration gave clear signals that negotiation of the FTAA would become a top priority. However, this could only become reality if this administration managed to overcome the domestic resistance that for four years had prevented the Congress from granting fast-track authority, which is now called trade promotion authority (TPA).

White House officials became very emphatic about their determination to win the cause on Capitol Hill, and the hemispheric agenda picked up during the Third Hemispheric Presidential Summit that took place in Quebec in April 2001. At the time, the thirty-four heads of state of the Americas agreed to complete the FTAA negotiations by January 1, 2005, and to ratify the agreement by December 31, 2005.

Brazil maintained an affirmative policy toward the FTAA, through it assumed a more critical position in the negotiation process. The Brazilian government stood firmly against the stance of the United States and Chile in favor of changing the inauguration of the FTAA from 2005 to 2003. Brazil also became an active player in the working groups in charge of the preparations for the trade hemispheric negotiations that emphatically appealed for reciprocity in hemispheric talks, stressing that it would not consider the FTAA an "inevitable fate."[22]

The granting of TPA by the U.S. House of Represetatives in December 2001 deepened discrepancies in U.S.-Brazil trade talks even more. The new congressional authorization included conditions that were considered unacceptable and were interpreted by the Brazilian government as an obstacle to further FTAA negotiations. Brazil became particularly concerned with two TPA clauses—one that previewed consultation by the U.S. government on currency mechanisms adopted by others if considered a threat to U.S. competitiveness, and another that listed 293 products to be excluded from negotiations, including an extensive list of agricultural goods. This meant that the United States could maintain subsidies for most of the agricultural products it exported to Latin America and would not have to touch antidumping legislation that restricted the entrance of many Latin American exports to the United States. Political leaders in Brazil, from the Left to the Right, and Cardoso himself, condemned the contents of the authorization.

On the other side, U.S. trade representative Robert B. Zoellick, who had been pressing Congress to approve the legislation since he took office in 2001, was elated about the vote. While business lobbyists shared this reaction, the TPA received no support from organized labor and was strongly opposed by the majority of the Democratic Party.[23]

In fact, it is possible to establish a correlation between the opposition to FTAA in both the United States and Brazil. The political motivations in each country are quite different, but they come from the most nationalistic political segments. In the United States, labor and environmental interests favor more protection and controls; in Brazil, the Labor Party and the nationalistic Right are against any kind of connection between labor standards and trade negotiations. In the United States, Brazilian resistance to FTAA, both earlier and at present, has been acknowledged by those more intimate with hemispheric trade negotiations. Former U.S. trade representative Carla Hills interprets the Brazilian reluctance as a consequence of three "challenges": lack of competitiveness of the national private sector, the concern that the United States as the dominating actor will not address Brazilian priorities, and the concern that the FTAA would curtail Brazil's preeminence in South America.[24]

Aside from politicization, very concrete interests influence the positions of Brazil and the United States in the FTAA negotiations process. South American markets have increased for Brazilian exports (from 11.8 percent in 1990 to 23.2 percent in 1995), and the fact that Latin American—and particularly the South American—markets have also increased their importance for U.S. exports creates competition between the United States and Brazil. On the other hand, the expansion of U.S.-Brazil intracompany trade has been reshaping the pattern of bilateral trade. Aside from the motivations induced by recent changes in Brazilian domestic policies, the increased presence of U.S. multinationals in Brazil has been stimulated by the new regional-oriented strategies it adopted to take advantage of the MERCOSUR process and would benefit even more from broad regional trade arrangements. This will definitely be a source of converging interests in the negotiations of a Hemispheric Free Trade Agreement.

Increased bitterness in bilateral trade disputes has contaminated both countries in their hemispheric negotiations. U.S. officials have increasingly conditioned specific trade negotiations on a broad hemispheric agreement, while Brazil argues the opposite, claiming that a regional consensus can only be achieved once the United States abandons the use of discriminatory unilateral trade policies. Harsh declarations by government officials on both sides have created a difficult environment in which psychological factors replace rational evaluations. If Brazil ends up taking a negative approach in the FTAA negotiating process, politicization of the negotiations process could escalate. Brazil represents a key player in this process, and its absence would affect the success of the project altogether. The maintenance of an active calendar of technical discussions, the preparations for new ministerial meetings and the 2005 deadline oblige Brazil to remain on the playing field. The scheduled shared presidency with the United States during the final phase of the process is also a compelling factor for Brazil to stay on track.

The ending of the Cardoso administration coincided with the beginning of the last phase of FTAA negotiation (2003–4) cochaired by Brazil and the United States. Even though the process involves thirty-four countries, both nations have assumed a greater role in the success or failure of the process. The Lula administration has acknowledged that dealing with Brazil's responsibility represents a major challenge in face of the strong anti-FTAA feelings shared by the political forces that sustain the government. On the other side, the Bush administration faces an ambiguous situation in which the recognition of the costs of excluding Brazil from the FTAA goes hand in hand with stances that reflect growing protectionism and less flexibility at home.

CHAPTER 3

U.S.-BRAZIL POLITICAL RELATIONS

THIS CHAPTER ADDRESSES A DIVERSE SET OF ISSUES THAT reflect the changing pattern of U.S.-Brazil political relations. Since the early 1990s, U.S.-Brazil political relations have undergone major transformations, influenced by simultaneous transformations in world politics and domestic Brazilian politics. As bilateral relations progressed, they involved new issues and complexities. U.S.-Brazil political relations are now shaped by a myriad of interests and pressures related to a diverse agenda consisting of issues that have become altogether more difficult to rank.

A possible, though not wholly satisfactory, hierarchy differentiates *first-tier* and *second-tier* political issues. The first is concerned with the state-to-state agenda, addressing world and regional politics and international security matters; the second encompasses the agenda of "global issues" set by societal movements, nongovernmental actors, and public opinion. The interaction between Brazilian democratization, on the one side, and the expanded community of nongovernmental actors attentive to world affairs in the United States, on the other, has had a major effect upon U.S.-Brazilian political relations. Though the erosion of the boundary between domestic and international pressures is a common trait in both first- and second-tier issues, it tends to be more visible in the latter.

The issues on the first-tier agenda deal with interstate relations. They include diplomatic affairs, as well as international, regional, and bilateral security matters, and evolve according to world events and crises in light of the permanent national security interests of both countries. Although the second-tier agenda also involves interstate interaction, it is essentially set by nongovernmental actors and interests. It is, by definition, an open and extensive agenda in which Brazilian and U.S. societal movements and organizations aim, in the first place, to broaden perceptions and approaches in bilateral relations and, second, to push for change in Brazilian state policies. The core issues of this agenda have been human rights and the environment. In both cases, there has been a permanent spillover into new and related topics, as the mobilization of different groups and organizations takes place. Immigration, media, and public opinion have also been included in the second-tier agenda.

THE FIRST-TIER AGENDA

Two aspects are crucial when focusing on U.S.-Brazil interstate political relations: the first relates to the a priori power structure to which bilateral relations are subordinated; the second refers to the bureaucratic apparatus where decision making takes place.

The most important shaping factor in U.S.-Brazil political relations is its asymmetric power structure. For the United States, the importance of Brazil in world politics and international security matters quite little, especially when compared to crucial allies such as Canada and Great Britain, to other world powers such as Germany and Japan, or even former enemies such as Russia. Yet, the reverse does not apply; Brazil keeps a permanent watch on the United States in world politics, and its foreign policy decisions consistently measure the costs and benefits of convergence or discrepancy with the United States.

In the post–Cold War period, such caution has increased in the face of unipolar world politics, particularly since the terrorist attacks of September 11, 2001. Discrepancies regarding U.S. intervention in world and regional crises have been discretely revealed in episodes such as the Persian Gulf War (1991), the crisis in Haiti (1994), and the Kosovo tragedy (1998). In all cases, the United States would have welcomed Brazil's full support. Even more, Brazil's choice not to join the U.S. bandwagon has contrasted with Argentina's full-scope alignment with the United States after the end of the Cold War.[1] Convergence between Argentina and the United States in international security and world politics was not only a factor of tension in Argentine-Brazilian relations but also helped to mislead official U.S. expectations toward Brazil.

Room for differentiation in international affairs has further diminished in recent years. In the post–Cold War era the influence of countries such as Brazil in world politics has been quite marginal. In its relations with the United States, Brazil's influence is defined by its relative importance within the American strategy of preserving its preeminent global position,[2] and Brazil's irrelevance within the American foreign policy framework limits the importance of hard politics per se in the relationship between the two nations. Naturally, Brazil would hold another position if its foreign policy would be more supportive of the U.S. strategic and political policies. Nevertheless, this has not been the case, as Brazilian foreign policy has insisted upon an autonomous worldview. Hence, state-to-state political relations between the United States and Brazil primarily aim for prudent coexistence, eventual collaboration, and minimal collision. While the United States moves ahead toward the consolidation of an uncontested power position, Brazil searches for a secure and legitimate economic and political platform in South America.

Though Brazil's stances in world politics have been secondary for the United States, the same has not been true in regional politics, particularly in South America. The United States has very slowly acknowledged Brazil as crucial for stability and peace in the area. Under democratic rule, Brazil has expanded this role as stabilizer/peacemaker, even though the government has repeatedly refused to transform mutual interests into a blank-check alignment. At the same time, the United States has become more open to the idea that Brazil should have a say in South American politics. Brazilian foreign policy, on the other hand, has also become less defensive toward the positive aspects of the presence of the United States and the pros of hegemonic stability. In recent years, convergence and cooperation between Brazil and the United States was particularly important in the Ecuador-Peru peace process and the efforts to encourage Paraguay's democratic transition. Security cooperation has also improved, especially regarding the prevention of drug trafficking.

It is important to keep in mind that there is a striking difference between the interbureaucratic realm in charge of bilateral relations in Brazil and in the United States. On the American side, interstate relations are carried forward by a bureaucratic mélange essentially conducted by the U.S. State Department, the National Security Council, and the U.S. Trade Representative. In Brazil, they are centralized at the Foreign Ministry, referred to as Itamaraty, which follows the general guidelines and political preferences made explicit by the presidency. Fine-tuning among the presidency, the Foreign Ministry, and the Brazilian embassy in Washington, D.C., has always been the bureaucratic mix that has taken care of U.S.-Brazil relations. In the United States, less centralized foreign policy decisions have on many occasions facilitated an unlinked negotiation process, unlike in Brazil, where the role played by the Foreign Ministry has stimulated a convergent line of action among different areas of negotiation. More recently, a particular effort has been made to use presidential diplomacy as an instrument for improving U.S.-Brazil political communications on global and regional matters.[3]

In the post–Cold War world, first-tier politics tend to follow a fragmented and less predictable pattern, particularly in the case of countries like Brazil, in which bandwagon diplomacy has been firmly avoided since the mid-1970s. Though the terrain for autonomous foreign policy has become more restricted, Brazil still aspires to retain some level of independent capability to determine its moves in world affairs. Clear examples of such aspirations include its leading initiatives in South America, the aim to become a permanent member of the United Nations Security Council, and its recent protagonism in hemispheric trade negotiations. There has also been a growing concern in Brazil to articulate political independence in world affairs with a more plural support at home. In the meantime,

Brazil has gradually adapted to the preeminence of the United States in post–Cold War world politics and security. Though it favors a multipolar world order, Brazil has become less defensive toward the unipolar structure of the contemporary international system.

The combination of political changes in Brazil with more recent world events has broadened the range of convergence with the United States, particularly regarding political values and world peace efforts. Brazil's reaction to the September 11, 2001, terrorist attacks upon the United States emphasized even more its affinity and attachment to Western political values. Brazil immediately voiced solidarity in grief as well as in broad-based efforts to combat terrorism. It also took the lead in the immediate call for an Organization of American States (OAS) conference, followed by the activation of the Inter-American Treaty of Reciprocal Assistance. For the United States, the role played by Brazil in calling for the OAS was recognized, though more action was expected regarding police and intelligence controls upon terrorist suspects at U.S. border zones. Nevertheless, subtle differences between the United States and Brazil emerged as U.S. military preparations unfolded in Afghanistan. At the time, the Brazilian government emphasized the need to avoid irrational reactions, and recommended caution instead of precipitated military response.

Ever since September 11, 2001, Brazil has developed types of approaches to face the new global security threats, particularly those involving terrorism. In multilateral arenas, most notably the United Nations, it has insisted on the need for a conceptual revision of world institutional structures, with special concern toward the humanitarian impact of military action and the importance of equilibrium between solidarity and globalization. Brazil's other response has been to enforce concrete domestic measures to deepen control over money-laundering operations that could facilitate terrorist operations, while the presence of U.S. intelligence in Brazil was expanded to improve internal security. Two months after the terrorist attacks upon the United States, Presidents George W. Bush and Fernando Henrique Cardoso met to fine-tune bilateral relations on world politics.[4] Brazil adopted a rather difficult position in which it avoided full-scope alignment to the U.S. defense policy and at the same time granted support to a U.S.-led war against terrorism.

World Politics and Security

Since the mid-1990s, Brazilian foreign policy has developed a positive agenda regarding the international security expectations of the United States, particularly regarding adherence to international nonproliferation regimes. In 1994, Brazil joined the Missile Technology Control Regime, and in 1997 it ratified the Nuclear Non-Proliferation Treaty. At the same time, Brazil has also supported the enhancement of multilateral initiatives, particularly the expanded role of the United Nations in world politics, while its increased participation in UN peacekeeping operations has meant that it has worked more with the United States in world affairs. Brazil participated in the UN Observer Mission in El Salvador, the UN Observer Mission in Mozambique, and the UN Mission in Angola (where it sent 1,300 soldiers, the largest military force it has sent abroad since World War II). Brazil also contributed police forces to the 1999 UN peace operation in East Timor.

Building a positive agenda in peacekeeping, however, has not kept the United States and Brazil from holding different positions on a large stake of UN General Assembly resolutions, particularly those on disarmament and human rights. Table 3.1 exhibits the lack of convergence observed throughout the last decade.

The table shows that the number of times both countries vote differently each year on both subjects is noticeably greater than the times in which they concur. For instance, in 1990, U.S. and Brazilian votes converged only once on disarmament and differed on twenty-three resolutions. This same year they converged on four resolutions and differed on eight resolutions on human rights. It is interesting to note that U.S.-Brazil disagreements have been more frequent on disarmament than on human rights.

An illustration of the fragmented pattern of U.S.-Brazil interstate relations can be observed in their recent voting patterns in different UN environments. While their votes will tend to coincide in the Security Council, they rarely do in the General Assembly. This is because Brazil's international identity in the General Assembly is closer to third world positions, which usually contrast with those of the United States and other great powers. Politics in the General Assembly basically reflect a North-South divide, and Brazil has long been an outstanding player in third world claims. However, this profile changes in the Security Council, where in the first decade after the end of the Cold War, Brazil has been elected a nonpermanent member three times: in 1989–90, 1993–94, and 1998–99. Here, in resolutions concerning crisis situations, Brazil rarely votes differently from the United States.[5]

TABLE 3.1

United Nations General Assembly Resolutions Voted on by the United States and Brazil on Disarmament and Human Rights

	1989		1990		1991		1992		1993		1994		1995		1996		1997		1998		1999	
	Y	N	Y	N	Y	N	Y	N	Y	N	Y	N	Y	N	Y	N	Y	N	Y	N	Y	N
Disarmament	7	24	1	23	2	15	2	13	1	15	5	12	3	17	5	18	4	15	6	16	8	14
Human Rights	2	12	4	8	3	10	3	8	3	6	7	11	7	11	6	10	6	7	6	7	5	10

Note: Y = same voting; N = different voting
Source: UN Yearbook

U.S. and Brazilian officials have also agreed on the need for broad institutional reforms within the UN system, including the expansion of the UN Security Council (UNSC). The Brazilian government has made clear to the United States and other world powers its ambition to be one of the new permanent members of the UNSC if the number of seats increases. Though France, Germany, and Russia have already endorsed Brazil's candidacy, the United States has been more cautious, as this would involve a regional preference that could hurt the interests of other Latin American members—particularly Argentina and Mexico, which have not given up their own candidacies to favor Brazil.

In defense matters, Brazilian military officials have not left behind strong nationalistic feelings that contribute to a defensive posture in negotiations with the United States. However, after a period of great resistance, closer relations have been accomplished. Besides regular bilateral military exercises, the creation of a Brazilian Defense Ministry in 1998 met long-held U.S. expectations. A Bilateral Working Group for Defense was inaugurated in 1999, and Brazilian authorities hosted and actively participated at the Fourth Defense Ministerial of the Americas (2000).

The creation of the Brazilian Defense Ministry has in fact eased U.S.-Brazil understandings in security matters. At first, Brazilian authorities strongly resisted the idea, which in the 1990s was one of the issues on the shopping list of security matters in U.S. talks with Brazil. The resistance mainly came from the military, which would not agree to subordinate its forces to a single civil authority. However, at the start of its second term, the Cardoso administration finally managed to enforce the initiative, which immediately led to a serious debate among the military, academics, and politicians regarding the future of Brazil's defense policy. As the ministry took on the task of preparing a white paper as its first important mission, it opened an internal debate on defense policy. The result, in general terms, was that different positions were taken by the military, the Foreign Ministry, the presidency, and the legislative branch. Nationalistic and anti-American stances have been more frequent among the military— particularly the army—and in the Brazilian Congress, regardless of party affiliation. Less nationalistic and more cooperative stances toward the United States were shared by the Foreign Ministry and Cardoso.

Improvements were also made in U.S.-Brazil negotiations over sensitive technology. This had been a taboo subject for both countries since the misunderstandings of the mid-1970s, when the United States opposed Brazil's nuclear agreement with Germany. Twenty-five years later, an agreement was reached for U.S. companies to use an equatorial launching site at a base on the northeastern Brazilian coast. For the Cardoso government, even though this agreement did not give Brazil access to technology, it opened up an opportunity for the country to participate in the international aerospace market.[6] These negotiations helped dissipate U.S. concerns regarding the agreement Brazil had reached with the Ukraine for the supply of rocket technology, while Brazilian officials expected to start a more enduring relationship with the United States in an area that had been a source of mistrust for almost three decades.[7]

However, this perception was not shared by all sectors in the Brazilian government. Besides the resistance voiced by certain segments within the military, the agreement was thoroughly reproached in the Brazilian Congress, which rejected it. This was a clear example of interbureaucratic differences in which the Foreign Ministry pushed for a cooperative agenda with the United States, while the military held strong nationalistic positions that were also shared by the legislative branch.

Regional Politics and Security

Presidential diplomacy during the Cardoso administration became particularly important in improving communications with the White House in order to handle South America crises. Special mention should be made of the 1995 war between Ecuador and Peru, and the 1996 political instability in Paraguay.[8] In October 1998, the governments of Ecuador and Peru signed a peace treaty in Brasilia, finally ending hostilities. The peace talks were coordinated in 1997–98 by the Brazilian government in permanent consultation with the governments of Argentina, Chile, and the United States (all of which have been formal mediators of the dispute since the first Ecuador-Peru war in 1942).[9]

With regard to Paraguay, Brazil has constantly coordinated diplomatic action with Argentina to contain authoritarian setbacks. Both countries have made use of the prerogatives offered by the democratic clause in the legislation of the Mercado Comun del Cono Sur (Southern Cone Common Market, or MERCOSUR) to pressure antidemocratic forces in Paraguay. Tension reached its peak in 1997 when Brazil, together with Argentina and the United States, held back an attempt to overthrow the democratically elected Paraguayan government of Juan Carlos Wasmosy (1993–98). The positive communication between the United States and Brazil has also been helpful in clarifying the different positions each country has assumed toward the status of democratic institutions in Peru during its electoral crisis of 2001.[10] While Brazil adopted a more cautious approach, the U.S. government made explicit its support for the enforcement of renewed democratic procedures. More recently, a new opportunity for U.S.-Brazil collaboration was opened in Venezuela, where the political fragmentation led to an escalation of violence and turmoil.

The U.S. government has acknowledged Brazil's most recent moves toward a more leading role in South America, following Brazil's initiative to sponsor the first meeting of South American presidents. In August 2000, all chiefs of state of the region attended the first South American Presidential Summit, which took place in Brasilia. The agenda previously set for the meeting included five topics: (1) defense of democracy; (2) regional trade; (3) regional infrastructure; (4) information, science, and technology; and (5) the fight against drug trafficking. Gradual attempts also have been taken by the Brazilian Foreign Ministry to bring more life to the Amazon Pact, created in 1978 between Brazil and its Amazon neighbors, with the aim of putting together a cooperative agenda with Peru, Venezuela, and Colombia.

Nevertheless, however discretely, concerns have been raised in the United States regarding the possibility that a more active Brazil could assemble South America into a single bloc that would destabilize U.S. preeminence in the Western Hemisphere. As Brazil aims to become more active in regional affairs, discrepancies with the United States in regional trade and security issues tend to politicize U.S. hemispheric affairs, and the idea that Brazil could be forging a "unified regional front in negotiations with the United States" has gained impetus within South American diplomatic and political circles.[11] Hence, Brazil's initiative to call a South American presidential summit was perceived as an attempt to "blunt Washington's strategy in trade talks of favoring bilateral agreements in which it has the upper hand."[12] Meanwhile, countries like Argentina and Chile have also manifested more caution than enthusiasm toward Brazilian diplomatic moves in South America.

Brazil has been reluctant to follow the U.S. drive to revitalize its inter-American leadership. Though the essence of this agenda consists of a hemispheric free trade agreement, it has spilled over to other issues such as defense of democracy, regional security, and common social policies. In this context, Brazil has been perceived by U.S. officials and scholars as an obstructive actor that has impeded the United States from freely setting and commanding the agenda.[13] However, tensions between the United States and Brazil were more visible before and during the 1994 Miami Summit than at the 1998 Santiago Summit or the 2001 Quebec Summit. A plausible explanation for this is that the United States did not hold the same vigorous position at the Santiago Summit that it did in Miami, due to the missing fast-track authority needed by U.S. president Bill Clinton to carry out the FTAA negotiations. At the Quebec Summit, full convergence was reached regarding the political agenda, especially with respect to defense of democracy. Meanwhile, however, discrepancies on free trade negotiations became particularly thorny.

Brazilian foreign policy has always been emphatically anti-interventionist, but in the United States, particularly during Democratic administrations, the promotion of democracy in the Americas has always been an issue area immersed in deeply held convictions that may justify intervention. Though more flexible than in the past, Brazil still strongly stands for national sovereignty prerogatives, asserting that the internal affairs of a state should be the concern of each individual country. While commonalties have arisen regarding democratic values in

South America, Brazil and the United States do not always agree on the best method for promoting these values. The 2001 electoral crisis in Peru, as well as the 1994 crisis in Haiti, exposed differences of principles between the United States and Brazil in this regard that have also been at the center of the bilateral dissent regarding the continued exclusion of Cuba from inter-American institutions.

While the improvement of U.S.-Brazil relations in defense matters has taken place in a context of political relaxation, Brazil has assumed a more active presence in regional security matters. Concerns regarding the growing impact of the Colombian crisis led Brazilian officials in 2001 to participate with other international delegations as observers in the first open peace meeting held between the Colombian government and guerrilla organizations. Brazil also hosted a Latin American and Caribbean conference to develop a regional approach for the 2001 UN conference on illicit small arms traffic, which aimed to deepen security cooperation in the region.[14] Brazil was also put on the map by the United States for defense surplus equipment. As a result, six U.S. warships previously sent in a leasing regime were incorporated into the Brazilian navy.

The main source of difficulties in U.S.-Brazil regional politics at present stems from the delicate situation in Colombia, as growing U.S. military involvement in support of the Colombian government in combating drug traffickers and guerrillas has had a negative impact on the security conditions in the Amazon region near Brazil's borders.[15] Brazil is particularly concerned with Colombia's political future and the possibility that it has become tied to a deepening U.S. political and military presence.

Brazilian apprehensions have dramatically increased since the U.S. Congress approved Plan Colombia in 2000, which commits 1.3 billion dollars to fight drug trafficking in that country.[16] The connection between defense policy and the protection of the Amazon has increasingly led the Brazilian military, politicians, and government officials to fear the effects of U.S. intervention in the area. Meanwhile, the increased presence of Brazilian military on the border with Colombia has expanded budgetary needs and enhanced the importance of defense policy in Brazil's regional agenda. The Querari Operation, launched in 1999, became Brazil's largest military operation in the Amazon region. It involved 5,000 men with the collaboration of the navy and the air force, with a jungle brigade formed by specially trained indigenous soldiers. The government has also substantially increased the budget of the Amazon region's Calha Norte Project, which gives high priority to social work and infrastructure initiatives in areas inhabited by poor populations as well as indigenous communities. While Brazilian military and police forces have demonstrated their intention to assume defense measures against narcoguerrilla activities in the Amazon, they face a dramatic lack of resources to meet their needs.

New developments in U.S.-Brazil relations regarding regional security took place during the Fourth Defense Ministerial Conference of the Americas held in October 2000 at Manaus, Brazil. As this was the first post–Plan Colombia hemispheric defense conference, concerns were high regarding what the United States would expect of Brazil. Caution prevailed on both sides: Brazilian officials made it clear that they were not willing to offer support to Plan Colombia, while U.S. officials were firm on the need to expand action to curtail drug trafficking in the area.

Following the terrorist attacks of September 11, 2001, a major switch in U.S. security interests toward South America inevitably affected relations with Brazil. The United States wishes to maintain a positive agenda with Brazil in defense policies to assure the equilibrium of its security policy in the Southern Cone, in which the ideal since the end of the Cold War has been to combine military alliances with modest relationships.[17] The terrorist attacks of September 11, 2001, have raised U.S expectations of the level of response and commitment from its Latin American partners. U.S. security concerns vis-à-vis Latin America include new areas of collaboration, such as the strengthening of intelligence cooperation, regional coordination to face new security threats, effective counterterrorist efforts, law enforcement and judicial measures to contain criminal activities, and denial of any sort of support to governments that sponsor terrorism. According to the U.S. government, one-third of the terrorist groups spread around the world operate in Latin America.

The U.S. government has become particularly concerned with the need to improve intelligence and police control in the "triple border" area between the cities of Puerto Iguazu (Argentina), Cuidad del Este (Paraguay), and Foz do Iguaçu (Brazil), which the Federal Bureau of Investigation considers a sanctuary for Islamic terrorists. Mutual counterdrug efforts have become particularly intense between Brazil and its MERCOSUR partners according to the lines of the Triple Border Security Plan drawn in 1998, followed by agreements facilitating extradition and joint police operations. Special attention has also been given to the presence of money laundering, illegal arms, and drug trafficking activities in the area.

New tensions emerged between the United States and Brazil at the Fifth Defense Ministerial (2002) in Santiago, as a consequence of Washington's expectations regarding antiterrorist security policies in the region. Concrete military cooperation was proposed based upon three main ideas: increased cooperation among navies, coast guards, customs officers, and police forces to strengthen coastal defensive capabilities in the region, with special attention to the Caribbean area; regional peacekeeping initiatives articulated among Argentina, Brazil, Chile, and Uruguay; and effective initiatives to enhance the control over "ungoverned areas" that could become havens for terrorist action—particularly the triple border area and Colombia.

While the need for close collaboration on antiterrorist measures has become more dramatic for the U.S. government, the United States and Brazil have shared concerns regarding the repression of drug trafficking activities, which has been an important topic on the two countries' agenda since the early 1990s. The main concern on the part of the United States regards Brazil's role as a major transit country in which drugs are shipped to the United States and where precursor chemicals and synthetic drugs are produced. Drug transit through Brazil facilitates the movement of large amounts of cocaine from the Andean Ridge cultivation area to production centers in Colombia, and traffickers use "air bridges" over Brazil in order to evade aerial interdiction controls in Colombia and Peru. Traffickers also use the region's rivers to transport their drugs to Atlantic ports. In addition, drugs are transited from Andean countries—particularly Colombia—to Europe and the United States through big Brazilian cities, especially in the southern and southeastern parts of the country.

As stated, significant improvements have been made regarding U.S.-Brazilian cooperation in this matter. Formal collaboration has been framed in a bilateral narcotics agreement (1994), updated by a Memorandum of Understanding (1996), and the Mutual Legal Assistance Treaty (1997).[18] Apart from these bilateral mechanisms, U.S.-Brazil cooperation in counternarcotics activities has taken place in multilateral arenas such as the UN Drug Control Program—which Brazil joined in 1991—and the OAS Drug Abuse Control Commission. Together with the expansion of a cooperative agenda, the U.S. government expected to strengthen its presence in counternarcotics activities in Brazil by opening an office in Brasilia.

The U.S. government has also acknowledged that there has been progress in Brazil regarding police and legislative involvement in counternarcotics activities,[19] and it praised the Brazilian government for its approval of anti–money laundering and military air-interception legislation. Important institutional steps in this direction include Brazil's establishment of a National Antidrug Secretariat in 1998, and in 1999 the formation of a special congressional panel of inquiry on narcotrafficking, which is responsible for an unprecedented investigation into the connections among drug trafficking, money laundering, organized crime, and official corruption. Besides providing equipment and personnel for Brazil's Antidrug Secretariat, the U.S. government collaborated with this agency on antidrug and antiviolence educational programs.[20]

Brazilian authorities became altogether more open to improving their collaboration with the United States on drug trafficking controls. Following its hemispheric policy, the White House Office of National Drug Control Policy created a permanent connection with the Brazilian Antidrug Secretariat,[21] while the U.S. Drug Enforcement Administration (DEA) was invited each year to observe Brazilian Federal Police operations in the Amazon region. As a result, bilateral cooperation expanded, and the DEA also became particularly active in demand reduction and drug education programs, which includes preparing courses for the Brazilian Federal Police throughout the country, organizing seminars and conferences, and offering growing financial support for counternarcotics operations in the Amazon region.

In this context the U.S. government began to expect more progress in Brazil's drug trafficking controls, which involved creating more legislation, enhancing the enforcement infrastructure of the existing legislation, and expanding counternarcotics programs.[22]

There is a thin line between U.S. governmental assistance to Brazil geared at controlling drug trafficking and that directed at fighting human rights abuses, and U.S. assistance for police training and education in Brazil has targeted both problems. Nevertheless, human rights violations have mobilized a far more diversified group of nongovernmental actors and organizations in both countries. This will be addressed in the next section of this chapter.

THE SECOND-TIER AGENDA

The expanded presence of nonstate actors and interests in bilateral relations has upgraded the second-tier political agenda of U.S.-Brazil relations. This process has been connected to the politicization of specific issues such as human rights and the environment that are linked to "transnational advocacy networks," which have gradually expanded their presence in Brazil.[23]

Second-tier issues have increased their importance and political vitality as a consequence of the vigorous social movements and organizations in Brazil and the United States that shape international and local public opinion, creating new sensibilities, and nowadays affecting governmental decisions. While nongovernmental organizations have played a role in U.S. domestic and foreign policy agendas since the 1970s, their presence in Brazil is relatively recent, and a great number of these organizations are connected to the consolidation of democracy over the past ten years. They have improved their capacity to mobilize public opinion through the media and have become important in forming perceptions of domestic and international affairs.

Nevertheless, their behavior in Brazil has not always been welcome in government circles, and they were often suspiciously viewed as a new form of external intervention. In fact, international funding covers over 80 percent of Brazilian nongovernmental activity, most of it coming from bilateral and multilateral European agencies, religious foundations, and the World Bank. This suspicion has been greatest in the case of nongovernmental organizations (NGOs) that deal with environmental issues in the Amazon region. While these negative opinions toward NGOs may reveal a nationalistic overreaction, these organizations have also become, at home and abroad, a major source for criticism of human rights and environmental violations. Permanent media campaigns together with an expanded lobby activity in the United States and in Brazil have become the most effective instruments used by NGOs. Also, the five or six thousand letters mailed every year to the Brazilian embassy in Washington by U.S. NGOs and/or individuals asking for the improvement of Brazil's environmental and human rights policies give an idea of the daily pressure put forward by these organizations.

This section addresses two kinds of second-tier issues: those that are concrete, such as human rights, the environment, and immigration; and those that are less tangible, such as public opinion and perceptions, which may become a source of concern per se. In fact, perceptions and public opinion function as a political factor in democratic atmospheres. The relative importance of public opinion and perceptions and the influence they may have depend on the relative importance of the relationship for each side involved. For instance, perceptions in the United States toward Brazil matter more for Brazil than the other way around since perceptions in Brazil toward the United States have not represented a source of concern with the power to influence decisions regarding bilateral relations.

Second-tier issues became the most vivid political expression of U.S.-Brazil relations. The links between these issues and the consolidation and deepening of democracy in Brazil have greatly expanded in the last decade. U.S.-Brazil relations are stimulated by new connections between NGOs involved with human rights protection and the environment, growing Brazilian immigration to the United States, educational and cultural cooperation, and tourism. Furthermore, as will be illustrated, the question of public image, at home and abroad, became a concern for the Brazilian Foreign Ministry. The acknowledgment by the Brazilian government that U.S. public opinion could be an important aspect of its relationship with the United States reflected a more open worldview stimulated by the interplay of domestic and international actors and interests favored by the new democratic times in Brazil.

Human Rights

During the mid-1970s, human rights became a problematic issue in U.S.-Brazil relations. Because of concerns for global human rights, the U.S. State Department was mandated by law to produce an annual report on the state of human rights in every country. In this context, U.S. government tolerance for human rights abuses carried forward by authoritarian regimes in South America decreased substantially. Thanks to the emerging Latin American human rights networks, the U.S. official agenda became concerned with human rights violations in Brazil and elsewhere in South America.[24] At the time, NGOs were marginal political actors in world affairs, and the most important ones were connected to the Catholic and Protestant Churches.[25] Because of their ability to gather sensitive information, they became crucial channels for transmitting information in the United States about human rights abuses—executions, torture, "disappearances," and political imprisonment—committed by the military regimes of the Southern Cone. During the 1970s, the human rights movement in Brazil, as well as its counterparts in the United States and Europe, became as active as in the other Southern Cone countries, among which Chile became the most prominent in international networking.

Violations of human rights by the Brazilian military regime therefore became a sensitive matter in its relations with the United States and contributed to the deterioration of political relations between the two countries. According to the Brazilian military, U.S. human rights policy had become exceedingly interventionist, particularly after the administration of Jimmy Carter assumed office. Responding to the new U.S. legislation in which military assistance became conditional on human rights performance, the Brazilian government in 1977 unilaterally suspended the 1952 military agreement with the United States.

Two clarifications must be raised at this point. First, Brazilian human rights violations became far less important for the U.S. government than those practiced in other Southern Cone countries such as Argentina, Chile, and Uruguay, where abuses occurred in massive proportions.[26] Second, in the context of Carter's foreign policy, nuclear proliferation became far more relevant in the tense relationship between the United States and Brazil than human rights violations.

By the end of the 1970s however, this subject ceased to exist in the bilateral agenda, thanks to the gradual liberalization of the Brazilian political regime after the 1979 Amnesty Law and the changes made to its Law of National Security. Brazil was slowly put aside by international human rights organizations,[27] which concentrated their attention on the thorny realities that persisted in other Southern Cone countries and on the increasingly dramatic scenario in Central America.

While Brazil was temporarily put off the radar screen, human rights organizations in the United States and in Europe expanded in many ways. Throughout the 1980s, in spite of the difficult relations in the United States between the executive branch and human rights activists, their organizations' funding and staffing rapidly increased, as did the range of their programs and the scope of their institutional connections. Multilateral organizations such as the UN and the OAS began using the information gathered by human rights NGOs on a regular basis.[28]

As democratization spread throughout South America, the region's human rights agenda underwent major changes. By the end of the 1980s, military rule had disappeared from South America, and the peace process in Central America had enormously improved the human rights record in that area. In this context, the whole subject of human rights would go through a process of "refocusing and retrenchment."[29]

Confronted by the need to conform to the new democratic scenario, non-governmental human rights organizations diversified their agenda in Latin America and adopted an inclusive approach. In the early 1990s, approximately sixty groups were concerned with the Latin American human rights agenda,[30] which was no longer associated exclusively with authoritarian regimes but now with any context of abuse, discrimination, and/or injustice involving social, economic, and cultural rights.

While the defense of human rights assumed a broader connotation, it also led to more effective political mobilization worldwide. Consequently, the monitoring and denouncing of human rights violations came not only from governmental pressure but also from transnational campaigns. This changing nature of the human rights agenda was connected with the changing nature of the notion of sovereignty in world politics. The protection of human rights was now, more than ever, identified with a universal cause that disregarded national borders: the debate regarding the legitimacy of external intervention to contain abuse became more complex and subtle.

This change expanded concern for human rights abuses in Brazil where, under democratization, a new human rights policy had started to take shape. In 1985, Brazil became the thirty-fourth state to sign the UN Convention against Torture and Other Cruel, Inhuman, and Degrading Treatment or Punishment. Four years later, it was ratified by the Brazilian Congress; ten years later, Brazil announced its acceptance of the jurisdiction of the Inter-American Court of Human Rights; and in 2002 Brazil gave full support to the creation of the International Court against crime and genocide.

Notwithstanding these steps, in the 1980s human rights abuses began again to gain visibility in Brazil, with immediate international repercussions. At first, human rights violations were connected to the persecution and incrimination of peasant union delegates and Indian leaders in the rural areas of northern and northeastern Brazil. Following, human rights abuses were also detected in urban contexts involving civil and military police violence in the Brazilian penitentiary system. Local and international NGOs became active in denouncing all sorts of abuses in different parts of the country.[31] In 1987, Human Rights Watch of the Americas, the most important U.S. human rights NGO, opened its office in Rio de Janeiro and published its first report on human rights abuses in Brazil.[32] These abuses acquired an even more dramatic connotation as they also began to target children.

This scenario worsened all through the 1990s, when the number of death squads killing and victimizing street children and adults in large Brazilian cities reached unprecedented numbers. An expanded group of human right activists, journalists, church workers, congresspeople, and state prosecutors became particularly concerned with the degree of impunity these violations revealed. In this context, human rights abuse became a subject of extensive journalistic coverage in Brazil and worldwide. In the United States, major newspapers played their part as "essential partners in network information politics,"[33] and lengthy articles were published on the atrocities committed in Brazil against street children and the growing number of cases of military and civil police abuse.[34]

Since the 1970s, Brazil had been developing a human rights diplomacy to handle the pressures coming from the UN Human Rights Commission, the United States and various European governments, and international NGOs. In the early 1990s, coordination between domestic and foreign policy regarding human rights increased in Brazil in the context of democratic consolidation. The convergence between the contents of the Action Plan for Human Rights (1996) and the recommendations of the World Conference of Human Rights held in Vienna (1993) deepened this synchronization even more.[35] In fact, the "International Action" chapter of the Action Plan became its most successful part, as Brazil fully adhered to related international conventions. In 1997, the Brazilian government created the National Secretariat of Human Rights,[36] which apart from overseeing the enforcement of the Action Plan, chaired the government's interministerial Committee for the Defense of the Human Being.

U.S. and European human rights NGOs have fostered substantial financial support for their Brazilian counterparts. On the part of the United States, direct contact was established between the U.S. government and NGOs, which jointly became a permanent source of pressure upon Brazilian federal, state, and municipal government authorities, who have complained that international and local NGO activities impede fluent communication between government agencies and social movements. As human rights gradually resurfaced in the U.S. governmental agenda, particularly after the Clinton administration came to power in 1992, the administration was cautious not to include human rights on the list of the first-tier bilateral matters with Brazil.

It should also be pointed out that even though human rights abuses in Brazil have become a permanent subject of U.S.-Brazil nongovernmental interaction, this does not mean that the actors on both sides share the same perceptions. While concern in the United States tends to point toward the expansion of activism and the possibility of growing interference in the design and enforcement of recommended policies, in Brazil priority has gone to establishing closer connections between the decrease of human rights abuses and the enforcement of more effective social policies. Hence, Brazilian human rights organizations tend to identify the dramatic social inequality in the country as the main explanation to human rights violations.

While recent U.S. Department of State reports acknowledge government efforts to improve the human rights conditions, they also point out the overall limited results. A sense of disappointment is transmitted regarding judiciary action on police violence and the enforcement of local legislation.[37] These reports also illustrate the growing concern among U.S. and Brazilian NGOs toward the protection of two minority groups, indigenous people and Afro-Brazilians. The greatest problem faced by the indigenous population has been to secure exclusive use of the lands and natural resources of the reservation areas. Brazilian constitutional law is quite explicit regarding cultural and patrimonial rights in reservation areas. Brazilian indigenous policies have been a matter of domestic debate and transnational campaigns.[38] This mobilization has been motivated by two factors: the connections of indigenous rights movements with the landless peasant group in the northern part of Brazil, and the merging of indigenous rights with environmental protection in the Amazon region.

Indigenous movements in Brazil have expanded their political visibility in recent years. As interbureaucratic controversies have increased regarding indigenous policies, closer connections have been established between indigenous leaders and other "have-not" social movements, especially the landless peasant group. These connections became emblematic during celebrations in 2000 of Brazil's five hundredth anniversary, when indigenous groups, together with Afro-Brazilian organizations and the Movement of the Landless, used the opportunity to protest governmental policies. Whereas this kind of politicization is perceived by local authorities as a threat to national security, it tends to deepen the networking between the United States and Brazil's NGOs.

Afro-Brazilians have also merited special attention by human rights organizations, but this has been a more dubious question in Brazil. Besides the fact that racial discrimination has been illegal since the 1950s, there has been a consensus within the Brazilian elite that racism has been replaced by "racial democracy."[39] This is a new issue in the bilateral nongovernmental agenda.

The crucial part played by African American organizations in the South African antiapartheid movements allowed them to reach a new status as a pressure group in U.S. international affairs. Though this mostly reflects on U.S. African affairs, it has begun to affect relations with other countries with significant black populations, such as Brazil. African American scholars and NGOs have increased their interest regarding the development of Afro-Brazilian movements in Brazil. Perceptions are shared regarding the slow evolution of antiracist organizations and movements in Brazil. This has led to an expanded involvement of U.S. NGOs in promoting Afro-Brazilian affirmative action programs.

An interesting corollary of the growing connections between the African American and Afro-Brazilian communities has been the expansion of African diaspora tourism. African Americans have become increasingly interested in contacting other black cultures, especially those in the Western Hemisphere, and many believe that Brazil—and particularly the state of Bahia—offers a rare opportunity of immersion into a genuinely preserved African culture. The fact that Afican American tourists have demonstrated their concern with the Afro-Brazilian social reality has had gradual effects, particularly regarding the increase of black personnel in the tourist services in Brazil.[40]

The recent interest of African Americans in Brazil has also stimulated renewed reflections regarding the differences and similarities in both countries on the issues of racism and discrimination and the subtle distinction between race and color.[41] African American and Afro-Brazilian relations have gradually opened a new chapter in U.S.-Brazil relations that intertwine interstate and intersocietal connections; yet, government-NGO relations in the two countries have not always followed the same pattern.

Another interesting development that illustrates this difference took place during the preparations for the UN World Conference against Racism, Discrimination and Related Intolerance (2001). The governments and NGOs of both the United States and Brazil assumed divergent stances regarding the conference agenda. Yet while the main source of controversy for the United States was the demand for slavery reparations raised by African American organizations, Brazilian officials maintained their traditional position, which dismisses the idea that racism is a problem in Brazil, arguing that unequal social conditions are related to poverty, not race. In the end, more irreconcilable differences emerged between government and NGO representatives in the United States than in Brazil. While the U.S. delegation left the conference in reaction to the demands for past slavery reparations and to stances that condemned discrimination against Palestinians in the Middle East, the Brazilian Foreign Ministry improved the grounds of a "racial diplomacy" supported by the Brazilian black constituency.

Furthermore, in 2002 an affirmative action policy was inaugurated for students of Brazil's Diplomatic Academy (known as the Rio Branco Academy) that, if effective, could result in more black diplomats serving the country's international affairs and open the way for important changes in the conduct of Brazilian foreign policy regarding the question of race. Yet, distinct from the United States, affirmative action programs are still controversial within the Brazilian black community. A clear example has been the limited support from Afro-Brazilian organizations for a program initiated in 2001 by the Ministry of Education to increase the number of black students in the federal universities by way of a quota system.

The Environment

Since the end of the Cold War, the United States has expanded its profile in world environment discussions, particularly those regarding global climate change, ozone depletion, ocean and air pollution, and resource degradation. During the Clinton administration, global ecological damage was considered a threat to national strategic interests.

For Brazil, the growing importance of environmental diplomacy has been linked to both domestic and international political developments.[42] At the same time that democratization favored the expansion of Brazilian organizations engaged in environmental protection, Brazil became a target of environmental global campaigns.

The diversity of ecosystems and environmental challenges in Brazil created a rich and complex agenda managed by governmental and nongovernmental actors.[43] To face these challenges, the Brazilian Foreign Ministry expanded its involvement in multilateral environmental diplomacy in partnership with other governmental agencies and local NGOs.[44] While dealing with the international politics of environmental policy, the Foreign Ministry switched from a defensive posture to a positive environmental diplomacy.

Brazil's presence in the global environmental agenda is essentially motivated by the size and importance of Brazilian rain forest resources, particularly in the Amazon region. Since the mid-1980s, a growing mobilization of United States societal and governmental organizations took place, requesting that Brazil implement more effective policies to preserve these resources. U.S. environmental groups became an active source of pressure upon the local government as well as upon multilateral financing institutions, especially the World Bank and the Inter-American Development Bank (IDB), which imposed new conditionalities on funding policies.[45]

International environmental organizations intensified their moral campaign against forest degradation and the ineffectiveness of Brazilian legislation to protect the environment.[46] From the Brazilian official perspective, these campaigns were perceived as a path toward interventionist actions offensive to national sovereignty. The expansion of transnational campaigns against global warming and tropical deforestation coincided with the identification of Brazil as a target country, and Brazil was immediately affected by the inclusion of environmental policies by multilateral financial institutions such as the World Bank and the IDB. The extensive and continuous burning of the rain forest in the Amazon area during the 1980s had a negative impact on U.S.-Brazilian nongovernmental relations.

In 1992 the preparations for the UN Conference on Environment and Development, or Earth Summit, became a benchmark for Brazilian environmental domestic and international politics. Aside from the government's involvement in organizing the summit, Brazilian environmentalists initiated a worldwide mobilization to sponsor a global forum that attracted 30,000 participants affiliated with local and international social movements and NGOs.[47] Since then, a new impulse toward environmental politics has taken place in Brazil, and the involvement of the Brazilian Workers Party (known as the PT) in alliance with the Brazilian Green Party has strengthened the link between environmental and social demands.[48]

The approval of Agenda 21 at the Earth Summit set the platform for Brazil's environmental diplomacy, and specific policies were shaped to address "global environmental problems"—particularly those related to climate change, depletion of the ozone layer, and loss of biodiversity. Besides reaching an unprecedented status in Brazil's foreign affairs, environmental politics became responsive to new approaches, particularly those that underlined its connection with the rights of indigenous people and sustainable development.

In June 1997, Brazil, together with Germany, Singapore, and South Africa, proposed a Joint Initiative for the Environment at the UN General Assembly, which targeted the enforcement of Agenda 21. At the 1998 Kyoto Conference on Climate Change, the Brazilian government stood firmly for the limitation of emission of contaminating gases by the industrialized countries.

Meanwhile, the development of environmental policies by most Brazilian states expanded the grounds for the involvement of the IDB and the World Bank in the financing of sanitation and cleanup initiatives. By 2000, Brazil had obtained more than five billion dollars in loans from multilateral agencies allocated to environmental projects.[49] Moreover, Brazil became a relevant "green market" for U.S. exports of environmental technologies, goods, and services.

At present, environmental issues represent an important chapter in U.S.-Brazil interstate and nongovernmental relations. Since October 1995, official framework meetings are held on an annual basis to review main topics on the international environment agenda. The aim of these meetings has been to improve bilateral consultation mechanisms regarding the environment and sustainable development.[50] The effort to expand commonalties has been greatly motivated by an extensive agenda of multilateral conferences dedicated to such topics as climate change, deforestation, species extinction and marine degradation, and the prospects of a Rio + 10 UN Conference, which took place in South Africa in 2002.

The most important matter regarding climate change is the implementation of the Kyoto Protocol approved in 1996 to reduce greenhouse gas emissions. The approval of the Clean Development Mechanism (CDM) and the creation of a specific regime to enforce the protocol have become major concerns for Brazil, a country greatly interested in promoting the expansion of a CDM market. During the Cardoso-Clinton years Brazil held a less flexible position than the United States regarding the enforcement of the Kyoto Protocol, and imposition of controls upon the emission of contaminating gases by industrialized countries.

U.S.-Brazil talks on deforestation have been connected with discussions regarding the creation of the UN Forest Fora and the International Agreement for Tropical Woods (IATW). Both countries agree on the need to establish a broad regime for monitoring global forest conditions, but they have not agreed on what the scope of the IATW should be. Brazil thinks that such accords should include all sorts of woods, while the United States wants a more selective approach.

Even though U.S.-Brazilian governmental relations have shown noticeable improvement in environmental issues, it has been difficult for Brazil to shed its image as the outstanding "villain" of global environmental degradation. Continuous deforestation in Brazil has repeatedly damaged the country's image in the eyes of the U.S. public.[51] Aside from the gap between environmental legislation and enforcement, a step backward was taken when the Brazilian Congress approved a new legislation that softened the national forestry code.[52]

Under the administration of George W. Bush, the United States hardened its stance in the multilateral environmental arena. Furthermore, the U.S. decision to reject the Kyoto Protocol during the Seventh United Nations Conference on Climate Change (2001) was immediately criticized by Brazilian governmental officials. Brazil's position has become even more emphatic, as the Brazilian Congress ratified the Kyoto Protocol in June 2002, shortly before the World Summit on Sustainable Development in South Africa.

To summarize, even though Brazil and the United States communicate on a regular basis to express their positions regarding environmental issues, their stances hardly coincide. Brazil maintains that industrialized countries assume more responsibility regarding the global contamination while the U.S government is highly reluctant to follow other industrial partners such as the European Union and Japan in submitting domestic environmental decisions to multilateral regimes. Since the Bush administration came to power, these differences have increased. From a U.S. perspective, it could be argued that a similar reluctance is perceived in Brazil when the debate focuses on biodiversity. In this case, stances held by U.S. officials and NGOs in favor of more effective international controls in major forest areas—particularly the Amazon region—immediately produce strong reactions within the Brazilian government. Brazilian NGOs, however, are more dubious, as their position will also be influenced by their international connections and compromises.

Brazilian Immigration to the United States

The United States has become the main destiny of a new demographic movement created by hazardous economic and social conditions in Brazil. Though far less than in the case of most Latin American countries, Brazilian immigration to the United States has expanded more than ever in the last two decades.[53] Considered one of the most recent groups of immigrants to the United States, Brazilians have emigrated in search of improved socioeconomic opportunities. But aside from those who migrate on a permanent basis, many Brazilians come to the United States to study, the majority for postgraduate degrees.[54] As a small portion of the number of illegal Latin Americans in the United States, the Brazilian community has never been a source of concern or a matter deserving of attention on the U.S.-Brazil governmental agenda. The number of South American immigrants in general—with the exception of Colombians—has been far less than those who come from the Caribbean, Central America, and Mexico.

On the Brazilian side, emigration to industrialized countries has become a new issue for diplomacy,[55] and since the mid-1980s, dealing with legal and illegal Brazilian immigrants has become a major part of the duty of the many Brazilian consulates in the United States.[56] Emigration to the United States accounts for approximately 25 percent of all Brazilians living abroad. Though the data may vary according to the source, researchers state that the number of *brazucas*—the name given to Brazilians living in the United States—has surpassed 600,000.[57] Though the brazucas come from all parts of Brazil, emigration to the United States has been more common in certain areas.[58] Brazilians based in the United States live mainly in the metropolitan areas of Boston, Los Angeles, Miami, New York (including Newark, New Jersey), and San Francisco.[59]

Compared to other Latin communities in the United States, the Brazilian group does not hold a strong sense of community and its members usually perceive their presence in the United States as temporary. Though economic opportunities are a strong migratory reason, Brazilian migration to the United States is also motivated by the pursuit of better quality of life. Brazilians in the United States follow a diverse pattern regarding age, gender, and social background, though the larger portion is formed by low-skilled workers.[60] This has meant that many perform informal low-wage jobs in the American labor market, but these conditions are compensated by a general sense that living in the United States offers the opportunity to share improved citizen rights and a superior standard of life. Furthermore, while wages for unskilled work are considered low by U.S. standards, they are not by Brazilian standards.

Brazilians form an isolated group within the immense population of immigrants in the United States. Their social networking is based on family reunification processes and/or new links, especially by intermarriage, with U.S. citizens. Regarding their identity, Brazilians dislike being considered a segment of the Hispanic community. They do not live in the same neighborhoods nor do they develop acquaintances with other "Latinos." In the state of Massachusetts for instance, it has been "more natural" for them to establish connections with the long-established Portuguese community, which has had a strong presence in the area from the beginning of the twentieth century. Brazilian social networks and businesses in the United States are modest, and one can count no more than a half-dozen Brazilian "closed social universes" in the United States.

PERCEPTIONS AND PUBLIC OPINION

According to Brazilian diplomats, relations with the United States have finally achieved "political maturity." Bilateral political communications have become straightforward, and they avoid problematic areas such as trade disputes, which contaminate the relationship as a whole. There is also a strong perception among Brazilian officials that political commonalties have expanded ever since Brazilian democracy consolidated.

U.S. government perceptions are that Brazil, like the rest of South American countries, has made major changes that should contribute to strengthening the relationship on both sides. As stated by a U.S. government official in 1997, "The U.S. relationship with South America goes far beyond trade and economics, of course. Our policy in the region aims to keep the United States economically strong and internationally competitive, to promote the principles of democracy, and to increase the level of regional cooperation to more easily deal with transnational threats of narcotrafficking, environmental degradation, and international crime."[61] Yet in the United States there is a frequent perception among the public concerned with hemispheric affairs that "Brazil has a way to go before necessary reforms are deepened and institutionalized to the point that they provide a really firm, substantially irreversible guarantee of positive performance in the future."[62]

An evaluation of the relations with Brazil was prepared by a group of experts from the U.S. Council on Foreign Relations for the current Bush administration in February 2001 in which Brazil was considered "the fulcrum of any successful U.S. policy initiative in South America."[63] Relations with Brazil were perceived as essential to influencing the economic and political future of the hemisphere. This task force also acknowledged that to deepen understanding between the two countries it would be necessary to review U.S. policy toward Brazil so as to "work together on vital matters such as trade, drugs, and regional security and move thereafter to engage in a high-level sustained and cooperative strategic dialogue with Brazilian leaders."[64]

Among its most relevant suggestions, the report stresses the importance of understanding mutual differences and it urges the United States to discard a policy of benign neglect toward Brazil. The importance of relations with Brazil was grounded in four criteria: "economic power; its central location within South America; its status as a trading partner and the recipient of U.S. investment; and its diplomatic role within South America and the international agencies."[65] The study also warned both the United States and Brazil about the risk of missing the moment to build up a positive agenda. Though trade negotiations with the United States could be replaced by negotiations with the European Union, Brazil could not afford to lose preferential access to the American market. As well, both countries are perceived to play complementary roles in the promotion of economic reform and democratic stability in South America.

The Council on Foreign Relations report points out the challenges faced by U.S.-Brazil relations. Besides mentioning potentials, it also calls attention to difficulties, which involve five areas of misunderstanding: "the legacy and ambiguity of past U.S. policy toward Brazil; the fear in Brazil (and for some within the United States) that free trade in the hemisphere will harm them; the perception in Brazil that the United States seeks to diminish Brazilian sovereignty in the Amazon region; wariness both domestically and among Brazil's neighbors of too close a relationship between Brazil and the United States; and the elements of competition as well as cooperation that exist between both countries."[66]

The idea that U.S.-Brazil relations must improve is also shared by some prominent conservatives in the United States. Former U. S. secretary of state Henry Kissinger, for instance, has stated that both countries must make serious efforts to work on a special relationship; while the United States must treat Brazil with more sensitiveness and consideration, Brazil should consider a harmonious relationship with the United States as a foreign policy priority.[67] What Kissinger is suggesting is to a great extent a revival of the special relationship project he tried to enforce when he was in office in the mid-1970s, with adjustments for present bilateral agenda demands.[68] As with the Council on Foreign Relations report, Kissinger sees improved understanding with Brazil as linked to the importance of this relationship for a successful U.S. hemispheric policy. The main difference between these two prescriptions is the acknowledgment of the new complexities involved in this relationship, now especially concerning Brazil's aspirations and realities. According to the Council on Foreign Relations, Brazil experiences a vivid process of democratization that in addition to stimulating the broadening of domestic interests and pressures expands the legitimacy of Brazilian international ambitions in world and regional affairs. Accordingly, this reality should be interpreted by the United States as an opportunity to work together with Brazil.

Comparative perspective can be quite useful to grasp what makes U.S.-Brazil relations unique in the hemispheric environment. While complex, these bilateral relations have revealed more continuity than change when compared, for instance, with U.S.-Mexico relations. This kind of comparison was developed by Peter Hakim, who merited pointing out the obstacles the United States and Brazil face in improving their relationship. Besides enumerating past and present examples of bilateral cooperation and solidarity, Hakim briefly describes the aims and goal of Brazilian foreign policy and calls attention to the domestic and regional constraints the country faces. He points out that while the expectations regarding a full-scope understanding between both countries could become frustrating, it would also be misleading to expect a conflictive outcome. Hakim underlines the reasons why the U.S. government should adopt a cautious approach toward Brazil, considering that it could become counterproductive to treat this country as an adversary. According to Hakim, "the United States should be prepared to work hard to find common ground with Brazil, especially on trade matters. U.S. officials know they need Brazil's backing to make headway on many issues in hemispheric affairs. Brazil may not be powerful enough to fully shape regional policies to its liking, but it has sufficient size and clout to keep the United States from achieving its goals in such crucial areas as the FTAA and Colombia."[69]

The Brazilian government has become more conscious of the connections between the perceptions in the United States on bilateral relations and those regarding the country per se. A growing concern has emerged regarding the need to better the image of the country among the different segments of American public opinion. This has been the aim of the Brazil Information Center, linked to the Brazilian embassy in Washington, D.C., in charge of promoting a positive image of Brazil to U.S. business sectors. Besides the expansion of "made in Brazil" products, this center has also been trying to improve the competitiveness of Brazilian firms in the U.S. business environment.

Furthermore, in an effort to comprehensively appraise "Americans' overall understanding of Brazil," to correct misperceptions and enhance positive images of Brazil, and to "assist in planning and implementing programs in the international arena," in 2001 the Brazilian Ministry of Foreign Relations hired the National Opinion Research Center (NORC) at the University of Chicago to conduct a thorough study that would appraise "Americans overall understanding of Brazil."[70] Carrying out a well-planned, unbiased, and thought-provoking political-science study required dividing the American public into three separate population samples: the general public; opinion makers; and official, private sector, and academic concerns involved in U.S.-Brazil relations.

The main findings among the general public included very little knowledge of Brazil and confusion with other Latin American countries, though not on certain issues such as immigration and drug trafficking. Furthermore, "more informed respondents generally hold more negative impressions of Brazil than less informed respondents." Opinion makers, on the other hand, were generally more positive and more informed about Brazil than the general public. For their part, the Brazil experts were well informed about their particular areas of expertise, though not necessarily about other issues.

NORC researchers also suggested five major goals for Brazil's Foreign Ministry that had to do with publicity and public relations: an increase in information; image management; outreach to sectors of American elite; in-country support; and ongoing assessment of progress. Recommendations were that the Foreign Ministry must first and foremost provide more information to Americans about Brazil, particularly to both Democratic and Republican members of Congress. The survey also emphasized the importance of tourism as a means of exposure and connection between Brazil and the United States. Additionally, efforts were to be made to correct a somewhat negative image on issues such as economic instability, environmental degradation, and human rights violations—issues that are very common in the U.S. media.

On Brazil's side, perceptions regarding the United States usually involve defensive considerations. Governmental and nongovernmental actors share the idea that the United States represents more a source of concern than of opportunity for the country, and that U.S. hegemony imposes more costs than benefits. The U.S. presence as a superpower has been a fact of life for Brazil since the end of World War II, and throughout the second half of the twentieth century the United States was perceived by Brazilian elites as the most important power factor in world affairs. The strategic constraints imposed by a bipolar system downplayed the identification of the United States as an adversary, though in many occasions more was expected regarding economic support for Brazil. Hence, anti-American sentiments have been linked mostly to economic nationalism.

Nevertheless, the emergence of new international and domestic realities have reshaped perceptions in Brazil. A combination of contributing factors should be pointed out: the end of the Cold War, the expansion of economic exposure caused by financial and trade globalization, and the growing importance of domestic public opinion as a consequence of the deepening of democracy. In this context, the consolidation of U.S. leadership in the world since the end of the Cold War has deepened concerns among political, bureaucratic, academic, business, and social organizations as well as the military in Brazil. In the Foreign Ministry the dominant perception is that a multipolar world order, sustained upon effective and bilateral institutions, would offer more opportunities and fewer constraints than the present unipolar momentum based on U.S. primacy.

However, it is important to state that the most critical perceptions vis-à-vis the United States do not come from diplomatic circles. From the point of view of the Brazilian Foreign Ministry, if U.S.-Brazil discrepancies emerge, they ought to be managed, and conflict be avoided. According to Foreign Ministry perceptions, it is more important to expand responsibilities and international prestige in the world arena than to escalate a conflictive agenda with the United States.

The Brazilian media transmits a broad anti-American sentiment that expresses the views of different ideological preferences accompanied by strong nationalistic feelings.[71] It is in nongovernmental circles that one finds most antagonistic perceptions toward the United States, particularly within social movements and academic environments where leftist political thinking have experienced a major expansion. At the same time, democratization has stimulated a new interest within Brazilian political society regarding international affairs. Preserving an autonomous interpretation of democratic values, market economy rules, and national security interests are viewed as an aspiration that collides with the interests of the United States. This kind of vision has been shared by intellectuals such as Helio Jaguaribe, one of the most respected sociologists in Brazil, who is outstanding for more than fifty years as an advocate of Brazilian national interests. According to Jaguaribe, U.S.-Brazil confrontation will be inevitable in the near future since Brazil should not accept subordination to U.S. "imperial unilateralism." Yet Jaguaribe does not envision an "antagonistic confrontation," as he states could be expected in the case of China, but instead an "autonomy-driven confrontation."[72]

In Brazil, globalization and U.S. economic interests are frequently perceived as the same, viewed as being equally harmful. Hence, from a Brazilian perspective, apprehensions regarding U.S. post–Cold War leadership have been linked to a critical vision of globalization.[73]

It is highly unlikely that these sentiments will decrease in the next years in face of the hard-line foreign policy decisions in world politics undertaken by the Bush administration together with the growing pressures coming from the Free Trade Agreement for the Americas negotiations. In fact, these sentiments have been magnified by the U.S.-led war against Afghanistan, the expansion of unilateralism in U.S. trade policies, and by the recent war against Iraq.[74]

CHAPTER 4

BALANCE AND PERSPECTIVES

THIS BOOK HAS TRIED TO OFFER AN OVERVIEW OF U.S.–BRAZIL relations in the twentieth century. Its primary concern has been the coverage of the broad range of issues that shape U.S.–Brazil economic and political relations in the last decade. While these issues may appear to transmit a fragmented reality, they also reveal a vivid process of agenda diversification involving governmental and nongovernmental interests; their impact has not necessarily been the same for both countries, however, as these issues affect the United States and Brazil quite differently.

The main purpose of the previous chapters has been to point out that even though U.S.-Brazil relations have become more complex and diverse, the relationship tends to repeat the same pattern of (mis)understanding and mutual frustration. When compared with relations thirty years ago, economic relations at present involve a multifaceted set of trade negotiations and financial/monetary pressures. As delineated in chapter 2, bilateral trade developments have become particularly intertwined with multilateral trade disputes carried forward within the World Trade Organization and in regional trade negotiations. Political relations have also become more diverse, as we have seen in chapter 3. First-tier issues involve interstate relations dealing with international and regional politics and security, and second-tier agendas include nongovernmental pressures and interests driven by a myriad of human-rights and environmental organizations. Interstate relations become more promising when regional politics and security problems are addressed. Nevertheless, it is not clear how far U.S.-Brazil commonalities can advance once Brazil tries to consolidate a political and economic preeminence in South America. The expanded profile of actors and interests involved in the second-tier agenda of U.S.-Brazil relations reflects new realities shaped simultaneously by globalization and democratization. However, neither the changes in the world order nor the process of democratic consolidation in Brazil have altered the vicious circle observed in U.S-Brazil relations in the last sixty years.

As expectations regarding economic and political matters are never totally fulfilled, they generate waves of frustration. Hence, one could detect a cyclical movement triggered by renewed waves of positive expectations. In Brazil, perceptions regarding bilateral relations follow a similar pattern to those applied to the country's identity, which combines the notion of uniqueness with that of a promising future. Brazil has repeatedly made explicit its expectations that the United States should acknowledge its distinctive identity both in Latin America and in the international system. As well, the idea of the inauguration of "new eras"—frequently applied domestic politics—has been recurrent in Brazil's relationship with the United States. Undoubtedly, change can be perceived in the different phases—alliance, alignment, autonomy, and adjustment—that characterized bilateral relations throughout the twentieth century. Yet in all cases, a basic pattern repeats itself, leading to renewed frustrations. It is also interesting to note that while responsibility for change has always been placed more on Brazil's side, unmet expectations are mutual.

At present, U.S.-Brazil relations could once again be initiating a phase of unmet expectations. The inauguration of the government of Luiz Inácio Lula da Silva in Brazil was strongly associated with the idea of change. Relations with the United States could be initiating a new stage characterized by more affirmative stances by the new Brazilian government.

The international priorities put forward by the administration of George W. Bush since September 11, 2001, brought in new security variables that will also inevitably impact the near future of bilateral ties. How much change is there to be expected in U.S.-Brazil relations in the near future? Probably less that both sides would wish.

"We shall try to share with the United States a mature partnership based upon reciprocal interest and mutual respect"—this was the only statement in Lula's inauguration speech, on January 1, 2003,[1] that referred to Brazil's relationship with the United States. Though brief, this message can be understood from two standpoints. A more concrete dimension relates to the shared responsibilities in the Free Trade Agreement for the Americas (FTAA) process through 2003–2004, as both countries cochair the ongoing negotiations. A more generic interpretation alludes to Brazil's recurring aspiration for political acknowledgment and economic reciprocity on the part of the United States.

According to the U.S. ambassador to Brazil, Donna Hrinak, Brazilian frustrations have a point, and their continuous nature leads to more frustration. From her perspective, bilateral relations could and should be more intensive and balanced. One major reason pointed out for Brazil's irrelevance in U.S. foreign policy, compared to that of China and Russia, would be its nonnuclear status. This insignificance worsened after September 11, 2001, which "moved Latin America behind the stage."[2] In this context, the ambassador's recommendations were that common interests be upgraded by both sides, particularly those regarding defense of democracy, human rights, hemispheric cooperation, and the fight against transnational crime and narcotrafficking. The major developments in bilateral collaboration in many of these fields have been covered in chapter 3.

Because it inherited the agenda of Fernando Henrique Cardoso's administration, it was clear from the outset that the Lula administration would try to make many changes to its relationship with the United States. Its first concern was to maintain close communications with the Bush administration. With respect to the economic agenda, more innovations are expected in interstate regional trade negotiations than in the relationship with the private investors, the banking system, and the Washington-based multilateral credit institutions. The FTAA negotiations will undoubtedly become the most delicate terrain for both sides.

To face this challenge, the new Brazilian government has adopted a twofold strategy. On the one hand, it will use the Mercado Comun del Cono Sur (Southern Cone Common Market) as its main shield to face U.S. pressures; on the other hand, it shall try to move ahead in the buildup of a South American free trade zone as a second-best solution if the FTAA as a unique negotiation tool fails or becomes too costly. The Brazilian government will also maintain a broad and thorough process of consultation with productive and social sectors at home to evaluate the pros and cons of a free trade deal with the United States. Thus, consensus regarding services, intellectual property, agriculture, and antidumping duties have become critical to defining Brazil's strategy in the FTAA process. At the same time, Lula's inauguration has generated new expectations on the part of U.S. labor and environmental groups that Brazil will become more open to including discussions for minimum standards on both topics in free trade negotiations.

Besides regional negotiations, expanding access to the U.S. domestic market has and will continue to be a top priority for Brazil. Even though increasing trade with the European Union—together with the deepening of links with Latin America through the stimulation of regional economic arrangements—will likely become even more important, the United States still represents a major target. In 2002, besides absorbing 28 percent of Brazilian exports, the United States was responsible for 42 percent of Brazil's trade surplus.

Regarding political matters, the differences between the two countries in world politics will tend to continue and even deepen regarding U.S. global strategic priorities. The Lula administration will maintain the same commitment to multilateral solutions as its predecessor. Affinities between the two will be more easily found in regional matters, particularly in situations where democratic institutions face serious risk. To a certain point, the coming to power of the Lula government has presented the Bush administration with an opportunity to recover a positive relationship with Latin American partners after a period of relative neglect due to post–September 11, 2001, security priorities.[3] On Brazil's side, the intention of assuming a more active role vis-à-vis political turbulences in the region has generated a new interest in maintaining communications with the White House.

In this context, the approach taken by the two countries toward the Venezuelan political crisis in the first months of 2003 became an interesting test case. This was the first time the United States had acceded to participating *inter pares* in a coordinated regional diplomatic initiative, while, also for the first time, Brazil took the lead in putting together such an idea. Labeled the Group of Friends of Venezuela, the initiative also includes Chile, Colombia, Mexico, Portugal, and Spain, as well as the secretary general of the Organization of American States (OAS). Its main aim has been to bridge the understandings between the government of Hugo Chávez and the opposition groups to find a political solution that would not violate democratic principles. Even though the concrete results may be modest, the presence of the United States and Brazil and the perseverance of the OAS have helped hold back the deterioration of the political situation in Venezuela, which could lead to civil war.

Nevertheless, a partially successful result in the case of Venezuela may not help reduce the distance between Brasilia and Washington, D.C., regarding other turbulent realities in the region. In fact, divergent perceptions and policies may deepen even more in the case of the war in Colombia. Of the many factors that contribute to differences in their stances, the fact that the United States links its participation in the Colombian conflict with the war against terrorism gives its political and military involvement a different connotation. While the U.S. government has contributed to deepen a militarized approach to deal with the war in Colombia, Brazil has made explicit its preferences toward a political process involving international mediation, with the participation of the United Nations, based upon the premise that all parties at war should participate in the negotiations. Undoubtedly there are major differences regarding the political and ideological affinities between the United States and Brazil that reflect upon relations with Colombia and Venezuela. Relations between the government of Uribe in Colombia and the Bush administration have been far more friendly and cooperative than those with Chávez in Venezuela, while exactly the opposite can be said in the case of the Lula government. Washington nevertheless expects Brazilian involvement in the Colombian war to expand and to adjust to U.S.-Colombia security priorities.

Finally, though this is not yet on the horizon, Cuba could become a new topic to be included in U.S.-Brazil political dialogue. While the United States will continue to insist on addressing relations with Cuba as a bilateral issue, the Lula administration could come to use its fraternal relationship with the government of Fidel Castro to talk the Cuban regime into a less defensive posture toward democratization and to persuade the United States to moderate the use of coercive policies toward Cuba.

While interstate relations between the United States and Brazil will tend to become even more complex, facing both smooth and bumpy roads, intersocietal links will expand greatly. As mentioned, democratic consolidation in Brazil during the 1990s has led to the boost of nongovernmental movements and organizations committed to human rights and environmental protection. One of the consequences of Lula's election as president has been the political strengthening of these groups' causes, both within society and government. Even though the international projection of Lula's leadership will be more meaningful for third world areas, it will also reach the politicized segments of industrial societies, including the United States. If social improvement becomes visible in Brazil under the Lula administration, this could become a new source of political leverage in third world areas and in the developed world. The inclusion of the social agenda as a matter of foreign affairs rapidly became the Lula administration's most important international asset. Linking its priorities of fighting poverty and unequal income distribution at home with an outstanding international performance became the new government's most innovative feature.

Overall, in the coming years Brazil will rapidly move toward building a South American leadership role, with the expectation of expanding its global presence. While it would be less costly and risky if this trajectory could avoid having a negative impact on Brazil's relationship with the United States, it could become a new incentive for both countries to identify common interests. For the United States, the fact that Brazil does not wish to offer military support for the U.S. war against terror could contribute to deepen their differences in world politics in spite of the common values that they share. Instead of offering full support to a global war against terror, Brazil asks for support to initiate a global war against poverty. While for Brazil this is more a question of priorities, it also signifies an implicit condemnation of the militarized solutions adopted by the Bush administration to fight terrorism. Whether both wars can be conciliated or will lead to a new cycle of unmet expectations is yet to be seen.

CHAPTER 5

THE UNITED STATES AND BRAZIL: COMPARATIVE REFLECTIONS

AN ESSAY BY
ANDREW HURRELL

THE RELATIONSHIP BETWEEN BRAZIL AND THE UNITED STATES IS fascinating but puzzling. Brazil is a country that, on a wide list of measures and indices, matters both to the outside world as a whole and to the United States in particular. It is the fifth most populous country in the world (with a 2004 population of 182 million), after China, India, Indonesia, and the United States, and ahead of Japan and Russia. It has the world's twelfth largest gross domestic product (GDP), dropping from being the eighth largest in 1998. It is the largest country in South America (comprising 45 percent of the population of Central and South America and contributing 51.5 percent of the regional GDP). Brazil's is the seventh largest economy in terms of services output, the third largest producer of meat, the second largest producer of fruit and of sugar, and the third largest producer of oil seeds.

Equally, it is not difficult to show that what happens in Brazil has the potential to affect both U.S. society and U.S. foreign policy interests. This is the case whether we are talking about tropical forests and the environment, about the functioning of the global financial system, or about the implications of political developments within Brazil for South America as a whole. Picking up an old line of commentary, analysts in the late 1990s identified Brazil as one of the "Big Ten" emerging markets, along with countries like China and India, which are "acquiring enough power to change the face of global politics and economics."[1] Others have seen the country as one of the "pivotal states" that will dominate future U.S. policy toward the developing world.[2]

And yet, there appears to be a large gap between such assertions of Brazil's importance and the actual character of U.S.-Brazil relations. In 1982 Albert Fishlow described the relationship as "missing."[3] As the chapters in this book have shown, it is clearly no longer missing; in some respects there has been convergence as compared to the 1970s and 1980s; and there is a clear agenda of

[handwritten margin note: may be getting closer the 1st ... check what are the ... presids Obama ... called or answered after winning and after taking office]

important issues of mutual concern that are not going to disappear. But the relationship is hardly close and has been characterized both by real clashes of interest (especially over economic and trade issues), by deep and persistent divergences in the way in which the two countries view the international system, and by a recurrent sense of frustration. During the 1990s it was common to find speeches and statements about U.S. policy toward Latin America that made no— or only the slightest—mention of Brazil. For some commentators Brazil just about made it onto the "A list" of U.S. regional concerns, but its relative priority was deemed to be well below that of Colombia, Cuba, and Mexico.[4] The phrases used to capture the changing character of relations elsewhere in the region ("inevitable partnership," "toward a hemispheric community") seem jarringly inapplicable to the recent history of relations between the United States and Brazil. Indeed, the tenor of the 2001 U.S. Council on Foreign Relations Task Force Report reflected the absence of an existing cooperative engagement and the lack of understanding of Brazil's importance to the United States.[5] The choice of language is telling as we read that "we should begin to listen to Brazilian perspectives and to consider Brazil as a major strategic partner" and "Brazil can be a serious partner." Such language both highlights the clear absence of an existing close partnership and hints at U.S. doubts as to Brazil's reliability.

The absence either of close concern or of sustained engagement distinguishes the Brazilian case from U.S. relations with other major regional powers such as India, Indonesia, or South Africa, and certainly from other large emerging economies such as those of China, India, or Russia. Even where, as in the case of India, relations have historically been tense or conflictual, there was little doubt in the U.S. government that India mattered in big and important ways. This has never been consistently true of Brazil. In part this distinctiveness must be seen as a function of Latin America's particular place within the broader range of U.S. geopolitical and geoeconomic interests. But it also reflects both the distinctiveness of Brazil's foreign policy trajectory and the particular way in which the U.S.-Brazil relationship has evolved.

Brazilian foreign policy has certainly differed significantly from that of other states in Latin America such as Argentina, Chile, or Mexico; Brazil stood apart from the general move toward the United States that characterized hemispheric relations in the second half of the 1980s and through the 1990s, most prominently in the cases of these three countries. Brazil adopted its own particular understandings of the dramatic changes in international environment that followed the end of the Cold War and the perceived intensification of globalization. It moved toward economic liberalization; but the process of economic reform domestically remained more complex and checkered than elsewhere. Many aspects of its previous foreign policy were altered; but the concern with power, national interest, and even autonomy by no means disappeared. It became increasingly prepared to engage actively within international institutions and to accept many emerging international norms on such issues as democracy and human rights, the global environment, and arms control; but it maintained the objective of re-forming international institutions to secure a greater role for itself and of building coalitions to promote its own interests. It sought to avoid confrontation with the United States and promoted improved relations with the U.S. government, but was reluctant to become too closely involved with many aspects of the U.S. regional agenda (for example, on drugs or democracy promotion), and sought to use regional integration around the Mercado Comun del Cono Sur (Southern Cone Common Market, or MERCOSUR) to negotiate the terms of a possible hemispheric free trade area (the Free Trade Agreement for the Americas, or FTAA). Moreover, as we shall see, Brazilian criticism of the international system and of the role of the United States within it grew sharper in the latter years of the administration of Fernando Henrique Cardoso, with every sign that this is continuing under the administration of Luiz Inácio Lula da Silva, which came into office in January 2003.

For some analysts it is precisely this series of Brazilian policy choices and the domestic politics and national ideologies inside Brazil that explains the distinctive character of U.S.-Brazil relations—and the differences between Brazil and Mexico.[6] But although such factors are clearly important, a relationship cannot be explained by looking only at one side. Outcomes in international relations cannot be understood in terms of the attributes and preferences of a single country, but only by examining the interaction of states within an evolving international context.

This essay is divided into three sections. The first section assesses different explanations for the pattern of U.S.-Brazil relations. It argues that, in contrast to the liberal accounts that were prominent in the 1990s and that carry considerable explanatory weight elsewhere in the Western Hemisphere, this relationship needs to be understood in quite traditional statist terms in which relative power and hard interest continue to play crucial roles. The second section considers two limitations or reservations to this rather stark power/interest account: the role of perceptions and the multiple factors that explain U.S. and Brazilian preferences. The final section examines the implications and prospects for the future of the relationship in the light of the election of Lula and the changed character and pattern of U.S. foreign policy following the terrorist attacks of September 11, 2001.

EXPLANATION

In the 1990s liberalism both as a political program and as a model for analyzing international relations enjoyed a resurgence. The themes are familiar: the end of the Cold War and the victory of the West; the spread of democracy and of market liberalism; the apparent revival of the United Nations and the more general move toward international institutions and global governance; and the belief that globalization was transforming world politics, fundamentally altering the content and meaning of sovereignty, the instruments of statecraft, and the policies that states are able to pursue, and opening up new arenas of transnational political activity.

The 1990s also saw a remarkable resurgence of liberal perspectives on U.S. relations with Latin America. Liberalism had long formed a central part of the rhetoric of inter-American relations and of the idea of hemispheric solidarity based around republican values, international law, and regional institutions. But for long periods it had been on the defensive. However, from the late 1980s on, liberal interpretations of inter-American relations gained ground, claiming to provide a more accurate account of the dramatic changes that have taken place in U.S.-Latin American relations. Reflecting core assumptions of liberal theories of international relations more generally, this way of looking at the region emphasized the increasing density and depth of societal, ecological, and economic interdependence between the states and societies of the region; the emergence of an ideological consensus built around a belief in market liberalism and political democracy; the emergence or strengthening of new actors within a more active and activist regional transnational civil society; the increased pluralism of policy making in both U.S. policy toward the region and within Latin American states; and the increasing importance of multilateralism and regional institutions that reflected the powerful imperatives to collaborate across an increasingly wide range of international and transnational issues.[7]

Moreover, even as the international scene grows harsher and more Hobbesian, analytic liberalism remains influential, with the claim that we can explain outcomes in international politics by tracing the influence of domestic actors on underlying state preferences.[8] Thus, many would argue that U.S.-Brazil relations have entered more troubled waters precisely because of domestic, unit-level developments in the two countries: the arrival of a strongly nationalist and unilateralist administration in the U.S. government, and the victory of Lula and of the Brazilian Workers Party in the 2002 presidential elections.

Given the prevalence of this perspective in both policy writing and academic analysis, this section considers five central aspects of U.S. relations with Brazil.

Ideological Liberalism

It is a central liberal claim that democratization will shift the objectives and priorities of foreign policy and, in particular, will increase the possibility of cooperation with other democratic states both globally and within regions. Certainly the success of democratization in Brazil and the spread of democracy across the region was an important element in the changed character of hemispheric relations in the 1990s. It also had generally positive repercussions in terms of Brazil's relations with the United States. The United States was happy to applaud and support democratization in Brazil.[9] Moreover, for Brazilian policy makers in the dark days of the 1980s, debt crisis democratization represented one of the few assets that the country had to exploit. As Marcílio Marques Moreira put it upon his arrival in Washington, D.C., as ambassador in 1986, "I only had one trump card—namely, democratization, which brought a new legitimacy to Brazil's position."[10] Since then Brazil has consistently stressed the importance of democracy in its regional policy and acted together with the United States cooperatively to support democratic government in Paraguay. And the centrality of liberal values to the notion of a hemispheric community is upheld just as strongly in Brazil as it has been in the United States—as, for example, when Cardoso appealed at the Organization of American States (OAS) "Democracy Summit" held in Quebec in April 2001 to a vision of an American continent "defined not by the asymmetry of power but by a community of values."[11]

Yet it is a mistake to assume that this kind of broad ideological convergence feeds easily or neatly into foreign policy convergence. While it may certainly place limits on the scope of conflict, it does not assure stable cooperation, let alone harmony.

In the first place, consensus over substantive values can coexist with deep dissensus over the procedural values by which a group of states organizes itself and through which shared values are acted upon. Thus, Brazil has indeed supported democracy in the region, but it has been reluctant to endorse coercive intervention in pursuit of that goal. This was clearly visible during the Haitian crisis of 1994 and in Brazil's policy toward Haiti at the UN[12], and over whether OAS sanctions should be used against President Alberto Fujimori in Peru. The very different views of Cuba and of how to deal with Cuba provide a further example of how generally shared ends can coexist with strong divergence over means. This problem is tied to the paradox of universalism that, *even when genuinely shared*, the successful promotion of "universal" values will often depend on the willingness of a powerful state to promote them and that their successful promotion will work to reinforce the dominance of that state. The coercive imposition of shared values (via conditionalities, sanctions, and intervention) under conditions of power inequality and weak institutions is bound to create strains and to raise legitimate suspicions. And it has certainly done so in the case of Brazil.

Second, there may well be agreement as to the importance of democracy and liberal values, but quite radical disagreement as to which goods from the liberal basket should be given priority. There is indeed a good deal of consensus within the Americas regarding human rights and political democracy—quite a strong and dense overlapping consensus to use John Rawls's language. But if the political values within that consensus are not ordered and prioritized, then there is no guarantee that conflict will not result. In the 1990s, for example, "liberal values" were understood by the United States and its principal allies in terms of freedom from murderous tyrants and in terms of democracy, elections, and political self-determination. Notions of economic or distributive justice and conceptions of economic and social rights were almost completely absent. The theme of global economic justice had been central to Brazil's third world discourse in the 1970s. This faded under the pressures of the deep crisis of the 1980s, with its inevitable introspection and loss of self-confidence. But it has returned as an issue in both Brazil and many parts of the developing world as the discontents of globalization have become both more evident and politically more salient. Similarly, it was a feature of the 1990s that the developed democracies were happy to preach the virtues of democracy and human rights across the world but were curiously un-willing to apply these same values to the functioning of international institutions. The importance of democratizing such institutions was a central feature of Brazil's foreign policy discourse in the 1990s and was focused on its campaign for reform of the UN Security Council and for its own seat on that council.

Third, there is the changing nature of the challenges facing democracy. If dem-ocratic backsliding were simply a matter of military coups and the failure to hold clean elections, then a regional consensus may be relatively easy to sustain. But contemporary challenges to democracy in Latin America have far more to do with the murky erosion of democratic systems ("authoritarian inclinations in democratic day dress") and the erosion of the social and economic fabric and in-terpersonal trust that sustains democratic institutions.[13] A similar structural change has taken place in the field of human rights. Thus, for example, "tradi-tional" human rights violations by high-level agents of the state have undoubtedly declined in Latin America with the move away from military gov-ernment. Yet sustained and in many ways "structural" human rights violations still occur on a large scale in the form of low-level police brutality, the murder of street children, rural violence, and attacks on indigenous peoples. In many cases the role of state authorities may be difficult to demonstrate, or may indeed be wholly absent, and the capacity of weak and inefficient state apparatuses to cor-rect these abuses may be extremely limited. Even assuming widespread goodwill, these changes pose major challenges both for the mechanisms of a regional human rights system and the possibility of political consensus on the collective promotion of human rights.

Finally, these problems are compounded by the inevitability of selectivity. Sometimes selectivity derives from national polices and traditions. Thus, the U.S. government expects the region to take its strictures on human rights seriously, while at the same time remaining aloof from the inter-American human rights system. Sometimes it derives from the government's difficult reconciliation of human rights and democracy with other, and often "harder" interest—visible most notably in the government's historically ambivalent treatment of human rights and democracy in Mexico.

For all these reasons democracy can be both a source of shared interests between the United States and Brazil but also a source of differences and even tension. Venezuela represents the most pertinent recent example. Whatever the exact truth of U.S. involvement in the coup attempt against Hugo Chávez, the perception existed in Brazil and in other parts of the region that the U.S. government's action and attitude both undermined the consistency and coherence of the region's prodemocratic stance and suggested that its commitment to the defense and promotion of democracy was less than wholehearted.

Institutions

It is undoubtedly the case that Brazil's relations with the United States improved significantly in the 1990s due to Brazil's greater willingness to accept many of the dominant norms of the post–Cold War period and to its changing policy in a number of international institutions. These changes formed part of the broader changes that took place in Brazilian foreign policy in the late 1980s and early 1990s.

Thus, for example, Brazil moved toward increased acceptance of international norms controlling missile technology, arms exports, and nuclear proliferation. Previously Brazil had opposed the nonproliferation regime and had also refused to become a full member of the Treaty of Tlatelolco (which prohibited nuclear weapons in Latin America). The shift in relations with Argentina both stabilized the bilateral nuclear relationship and pushed Brazil closer toward acceptance of International Atomic Energy Agency safeguards. This process continued throughout the 1990s. Thus, in October 1995 Brazil passed legislation placing export controls on nuclear materials and joined the Missile Control Technology Regime. In April 1996 it became a member of the Nuclear Suppliers Group and, eventually, in July 1998, signed the Nuclear Non-Proliferation Treaty. Similarly, in terms of the environment, there was a sharp move away from the defensiveness of the 1980s toward an acceptance of the legitimacy of international concern for environmental matters and of nongovernmental organization (NGO) activities (which had been previously often been denounced as subversive) and toward a more positive engagement in international negotiations, especially in the process leading to the Rio de Janeiro 1992 Earth Summit.

A further change occurred in the field of human rights. Faced with persistent criticism for its human rights record (especially during the military regime), Brazil had earlier tended to adopt a very traditional stance stressing nonintervention in internal affairs and the illegitimacy of NGO involvement. And yet, by the 1990s Brazil had moved toward a very active human rights policy in the international arena as well as toward historically unprecedented emphasis on the importance of human rights domestically. In June 1990, for example, Foreign Minister Francisco Rezek received a mission from Human Rights Watch investigating rural violence. In August 1990 President Fernando Collor unprecedentedly met with representatives from Amnesty International and formally accepted the right of the international community to monitor human rights and work for improved implementation. In July 1992 Brazil ratified the International Covenant on Civil and Political Rights. As with security norms, this process continued through the 1990s. Under the Cardoso government Brazil set up a department for human rights in the foreign ministry; it drew up a national human rights plan; there was intensive engagement with the UN human rights system (with visits of UN special rapporteurs on summary executions, torture, new forms of racism, and violence against women); in December 1998 Brazil announced that it would recognize the competence of the Inter-American Human Rights Court; and in 1999 Brazil decided to sign the statute of the International Criminal Court.

More generally, we would expect to see a relatively weak country such as Brazil using institutions both to promote its issue-specific interests and to engage a hegemonic power like the United States within institutional settings. In the first place, institutions provide important platforms for influence for emerging states by constraining the freedom of the most powerful through established rules and procedures. The Dispute Settlement Procedures of the World Trade Organization (WTO) were the most important single gain for Brazil from the Uruguay Round and, as earlier chapters have shown, it is noticeable that Brazil has become very active in taking cases to the WTO including those against both the United States and the European Union (EU) and those regarding such high-profile and politically salient issues as steel trade and agriculture. Second, institutions open up "voice opportunities" that allow relatively weak states to make known their interests and to bid for political support in the broader market-place of ideas. In some instances Brazil has been proactive, as in its campaign for a seat on the UN Security Council or, more recently, in the greater willingness of Brazilian officials to use the U.S. government's proclaimed commitment to economic liberalism as a part of its criticism of U.S. protectionism in steel trade and agriculture. At other times, Brazilian policy has been reactive and defensive, as in its attempts to curb coercive interventionism, or the use of force without explicit legal authority in the cases of Kosovo and Iraq.

Third, and related to the above, institutions provide opportunities for influence via what might be called "insider activism." This involves working intensively within the institutions: being a catalyst for diplomatic efforts; doing a lot of the behind-the-scenes work in organizing meetings and promoting follow-up meetings; getting groups of experts together to push the agenda forward; and exploiting what one might call the institutional platforms and the normative niches that create room for maneuvering and shape how problems are understood. Brazil's activist diplomacy at the Vienna Human Rights Conference in 1993 provides a good example of this strategy and of the rewards that it can bring. At Vienna it sought to play an active role as a "bridge builder" and was heavily involved in drafting committees and informal networking. Brazil's sophisticated engagement with the complex informal diplomacy of the WTO provides a further example.[14]

Fourth, institutions provide political space to build new coalitions in order to try to affect emerging norms in ways that are congruent with their interests, and to counterbalance or at least deflect the preferences and policies of the most powerful. Coalition formation has long been central to Brazil's search for both influence and protection and continues to be so. Thus, in the discussions on a Millennium Trade Round within the WTO, Brazil has sought to reassemble a broad developing country coalition in favor of pressing the countries of the Organization for Economic Cooperation and Development to fulfill their Uruguay Round commitments on market access before any new liberalization is undertaken, and to resist the inclusion of environment and labor standards in the trade agenda. But here the important point to highlight is the increasing complexity of coalition formation. Within the WTO, for example, agricultural trade, services, investment, intellectual property, and biosafety each involve overlapping but distinct coalitions. A natural ally on agricultural trade may take a very different line on biosafety and trade in genetically modified products. This is a very different pattern from the broad North/South coalitions that characterized the 1970s and that have begun to reappear in the post-Doha round of WTO negotiations.

Perhaps most evident and most important has been the idea of MERCOSUR as a counterweight and as a negotiating instrument with the United States.[15] This fits a wholly conventional neorealist pattern of subregional groupings developing in response to the hegemonic power. And it is an idea that has remained enormously influential in Brazil despite the absence of clear evidence that (outside of the very special case of the EU) regional trade groupings are in fact able to increase external bargaining power. Brazilian assessment of its capacity to bargain with the U.S. government was tied in the 1990s to the improvement of its economic situation following the stabilization of the Real Plan in 1994, but also to the apparent and growing solidity of its regional leadership role. Thus, Brazil sought both to develop a South American Free Trade Area (beginning in October 1993) and to develop an expanded political voice for the region. This increased willingness to play an activist, managerial role was most visible in the process leading to the Brasilia Summit in late August 2000 and in the accompanying rhetoric: more open talk about its leadership role (although disclaiming all hegemonic pretensions); the development of a specifically "South American" perspective on international matters; and a greater willingness to challenge U.S. policy more openly. Equally, the deep crises within MERCOSUR in the period since 1999 have adversely affected this aspect of Brazil's strategic vision. But, as we shall see, Brazil's commitment to MERCOSUR as central to its strategy of international insertion has remained intact, and has been powerfully reasserted by the incoming Lula administration.

But when we turn to the hemisphere and to Brazil's direct interactions with the United States, the picture is somewhat different. Brazil's direct interactions with the United States take place in a rather weakly institutionalized environment. We can think of a strong institution in different ways. On the rationalist institutionalist account, institutions affect state behavior by making it rational to cooperate and by altering incentives. Institutions affect actor strategies (but not their underlying preferences) by reducing transaction costs, identifying focal points for coordinated behavior, and providing frameworks for productive issue linkage. On a more cognitive or constructivist account, institutions are strong to the extent that they shift actors' understandings of problems and of the existence and character of cooperative outcomes (via increased technical knowledge), or they create processes of socialization by which norms and values are diffused. Actors come to internalize external norms via institutionalized interaction leading to changes in both interest but also identity.

Considered in this light, the regional institutions through which the United States and Brazil have interacted are indeed relatively weak. Of course, the OAS enjoyed a renaissance in the 1990s and played a significant role in the promotion and diffusion of regional norms, most notably in terms of democracy. Moreover, the combination of U.S. power and the genuine convergence of values and interests between the United States and Latin America allowed the organization to move into a wide range of issues that would have previously been unthinkable. Brazil was unable to stand outside of these developments. It supported some (for example, the importance of regional democracy); resisted others (for example, coercive intervention to uphold democracy); and been a hesitant and defensive player in others (for example, the regular system of OAS ministerials dealing with security issues). On regional security, the 1990s saw important areas of common interest and cooperative engagement with the United States—most notably with regard to the settlement between Peru and Ecuador. But Brazil did not support the institutionalization of regional security—nor indeed has the U.S. government after some enthusiasm in the early years of the Clinton administration—and it expressed serious doubts about escalating U.S. military involvement in Colombia and maintained a strongly noninterventionist position.

The FTAA process represents the most strongly institutionalized arena for relations between the United States and Brazil, with its clear set of guiding norms and values, its network of working groups, its prescheduled ministerial meetings, its supporting network of technical specialists, and its links to formal institutions such as the OAS and the Inter-American Development Bank. This ongoing process has affected state strategies in a number of ways: by shaping understandings of what is involved in the FTAA and what state interests are; by diffusing economic norms as part of what one might call "the politics of the queue" (unilateral policy shifts to move ahead of other countries); and by shaping the character and scope of bargaining.

As the prospect of the FTAA appeared, Brazil placed primary emphasis on MERCOSUR rather than on the possibility of joining an expanded North American Free Trade Agreement (NAFTA), in contrast to Chile and Argentina. As the FTAA process became established after 1994, Brazil adopted a defensive agenda, stressing the need for gradualism and respect for national positions. From the Santiago Summit in 1997 Brazil assumed a more overt leadership role in defense of the MERCOSUR position and negotiated successfully on establishing the procedural ground rules for the FTAA process—the idea that MERCOSUR should negotiate as a single bloc; the necessity of consensus and of a single undertaking; the inclusion of all sectors; the importance of compatibility with WTO norms, the coexistence between FTAA and regional trade arrangements; and the continuation of negotiations until 2005. The failure of the Clinton administration to secure congressional approval of "fast-track" authority fitted well with Brazil's gradualist approach and meant that the 1990s witnessed a degree of "shadow boxing" rather than major engagement and serious conflict. Just as crucial as what Brazil did is what it did not do. Thus, we need to underscore the almost complete absence in the case of Brazil of the motivation that was so central to Mexico's thinking on the NAFTA: the idea of external institutionalization as a means of "locking-in" domestic economic reform.

There are many complex issues that face the United States and Brazil within the context of the FTAA, but two stand out. The first concerns the direct costs and benefits to both the United States and Brazil of the FTAA. Here we need to stress the high levels of uncertainty and the inherent difficulty of calculating the costs and benefits of "deep integration" projects.[16] Although the achievement of trade promotion authority (TPA) opens up the scope for negotiation (see the third section of this chapter), the outcome of specific bargaining is very hard to predict. What we can note are the very serious difficulties that stand in the way of success and the degree to which Brazilian views of the minimal conditions for a satisfactory bargain hardened in the period after 1999. Thus as Cardoso commented in Quebec in 2001, "A Free Trade Area of the Americas is welcome if its creation is a step toward providing access to more dynamic markets; if it indeed leads to common antidumping rules; if it reduces nontariff barriers; if it prevents protectionist distortion of sound sanitary norms; and if, while protecting intellectual property, it also furthers the technological capabilities of our people; and also if it goes beyond the Uruguay Round to redress the inequalities resulting from those negotiations, particularly with regard to agriculture. Otherwise, it would be irrelevant or, worse, undesirable."[17]

Second, there is the Brazilian goal of securing a rule-governed structure of economic relations with the United States—the extent to which the FTAA would protect Brazil and other weaker states from the use of the instruments of U.S. trade protection such as tariff peaks, antidumping, and countervailing duties. This is in many ways far more important than the direct balance of costs and benefits and is underappreciated within the Brazilian debate. The case of Mexico and the NAFTA highlights that, even under conditions of extreme power asymmetry, formal disciplines can prove effective. The difficulty for Brazil lies in gauging how far this outcome follows from the still unique and very special character of U.S. interests in Mexico.

One of the most serious foreign-policy dilemmas for intermediate states such as Brazil is how to keep the powerful engaged, how to press for what they want and to resist the things that they don't like, but to do this in such a way as not to place too much strain on still weak institutional or cooperative structures, nor to push the powerful to walk away. Managing this dilemma may often involve unpleasant concessions to the special interests or unilateralist impulses of the strong. The alternative is likely to be unconstrained unilateralism. It is this logic of hegemonic deference that explains much Brazilian thinking and policy toward hemispheric regionalism—and indeed to international institutions more generally.

But, whatever Brazil's own attitude toward institutions, its calculations and choices are made far harder by the ambivalence of U.S. policy toward the institutionalization of relations with South America. The 1990s did see a very important increase in the scope, range, and activity of regional institutions, and the U.S. government certainly did seek to use regional institutions to promote its interests and values (in trade and economics, in the promotion of political democracy, and in the ever-increasing range of issues included in hemispheric agendas following the 1994 Miami Summit). And yet, the incentives for the U.S. government to engage in regional institutions are relatively weak. Thus, when we look below Mexico and the Caribbean, regional interdependencies may be increasing, but they are not such as to appear manageable only through the creation and maintenance of effective institutions. Latin American states have far fewer resources to offer, compared to, say, Europe; and the U.S. government has a range of other policy choices, including ad hoc coalitions of the willing with multilateral endorsement; bilateralism (as in the case of Plan Colombia), unilateralism, and the extraterritorial application of U.S. laws and practices. Latin American states are relatively weak and are far more heavily dependent on the United States than the United States is on them. There is, then, little need for the United States to soften its goals or to engage in active multilateralism in order to mollify potential geopolitical rivals—the logic of hegemonic self-restraint that was visible in U.S. foreign policy toward other parts of the world in the 1990s. Finally, although the

United States has many unavoidable issues within the region, its global strategy and the widely shared need for the country to maintain its long-term global preponderance have not pressed the United States toward deep and consistent engagement in the region—certainly outside of Mexico. Indeed, U.S. power, influence, and autonomy are arguably maximized by refusing to become unconditionally committed to any particular region. Being partially in and partially out, making rhetorical gestures of commitment that are often at odds with actual policy, and sending mixed messages may all work to U.S. advantage. They may well help, for example, to prevent regional states from organizing themselves in effective subregional arrangements.

Pluralism and Foreign Policy

It is widely argued that the long-standing pluralism of U.S. foreign policy-making has increased, particularly in relation to the hemisphere. In the first place, increased levels of societal, economic, and environmental interdependence between the United States and Latin America erode the boundary between domestic and foreign policy issues, increase the salience of "intermestic" issues, and empower and involve an increasing range of domestic organizations and interest groups seeking to influence U.S. policy.[18] Second, the end of the Cold War ended the previous disciplining logic and organizing principles, throwing open the definition of the "national interest" in relation to the region. And third, the sheer extent of U.S. power and superiority meant that the United States could afford to have any policy or no policy. The trade negotiations, and in particular the negotiation of NAFTA, can be seen as emblematic of this increasingly central pluralist reality.[19]

The pluralist character of U.S. foreign, and especially foreign economic, policy is evident.[20] What Brazilian ambassador needs to be reminded of the centrality of the U.S. Trade Representative (USTR), the Treasury and the Federal Reserve, or of the complexities of U.S. congressional politics? And yet the image of pluralist, domestically driven foreign and foreign economic policy toward Brazil needs some qualification.

In the first place, the range of interest groups and lobbies is narrower and far less activist than in relation to that of Mexico and the Caribbean. Second, although there has been disagreement between successive U.S. administrations and the U.S. Congress over trade policy toward Brazil (most notably in terms of securing fast-track authority/TPA), this should not hide the very substantial overlap of interests and perspectives. The assumption that the United States should press Brazil toward further liberalization, the perceived benefits of playing economic hardball with Brazil, and the perception of Brazil as a "problem" and a "laggard" have all been very widely shared within U.S. political and business circles. Put another way, even without lobbying from affected industries or interest groups, U.S. foreign economic policy toward Brazil is unlikely to have been very different.

Third, the complexity of U.S. domestic politics has power-political implications that, in general, work to favor the United States. As theorists of two-level games remind us, "the stronger a state is in terms of autonomy from domestic pressures, the weaker its relative bargaining position internationally."[21] Indeed the compromise that emerged in August 2002 from the TPA is one that works well to strengthen U.S. bargaining power: trade promotion authority for the administration that will enable the resumption of serious negotiations on the one hand, but combined with an obligation to consult with Congress throughout the negotiation process on the other.

On some liberal accounts, pluralism within the United States is crucial because it affects the whole character of the country's hegemonic role and the way in which U.S. power is perceived by weaker states. As Daniel Deudney and G. John Ikenberry put it, "A distinctive feature of the American state is its decentralized structure, which provides numerous points of access to competing groups—both domestic and foreign. When a hegemonic state is liberal, the subordinate actors in the system have a variety of channels and mechanisms for registering their interests with the hegemon."[22]

This view correctly identifies a new and increasingly important face or arena of U.S.-Brazil relations, with Brazil coming relatively late (compared to, say, Mexico or South Korea) into the game of playing Washington, D.C., Beltway politics. But it must be doubted that this transparency, the diffusion of power into many hands, and the multiple points of access to policy making has done very much to balance, let alone to equalize, power relations between the two countries.

What of Brazil? The country's foreign and foreign economic policies have long been associated with a strong and relatively autonomous state and with rather weak input from political parties, business, or other societal groups. Moreover, Brazilian foreign policy in the period after 1985 appears to go against the expectations that democratization and economic liberalization will lead to an increase in the pluralism of the foreign policy-making process and a greater role for societal actors (firms, parties, and social movements).[23] The Brazilian state, in general, remained a surprisingly effective gatekeeper between the worlds of foreign and domestic policy, and Itamaraty, despite many predictions, has maintained its general position in foreign policy, including in relation to trade negotiations. Thus, whether we are talking about the Uruguay Round or the early phases of MERCOSUR, the input of societal groups or business interests was more limited than many predicted, and society-centered or coalitional accounts of Brazilian economic or foreign policy remained unconvincing. Although civil society in Brazil is highly developed, its access points into the political system remain limited, while business organizations suffer from many collective-action problems. Indeed, much recent literature has underlined the limited influence of business and interest groups over economic policy.[24]

However, it is very important to note the degree to which the FTAA has represented a change in this inherited pattern. There has indeed been a very significant degree of societal and political mobilization around the FTAA inside Brazil. Four factors explain this. First, the intrinsic character of the FTAA and the symbolically charged linkage between liberalization and alignment with the United States make such politicization inevitable—as with negotiations with the International Monetary Fund (IMF) and debt management in the mid-1980s or the nationalization of foreign firms in the 1950s and early 1960s. Second, and more important, there are the structural changes that have taken place in the nature of global economic regulation: the FTAA, just like the WTO, ceased long ago to be merely about trade. It contains detailed and deeply intrusive regulations on many aspects of what had previously been domestic economic management. Equally, in the old days of the General Agreement on Tariffs and Trade, states had merely to refrain from certain actions contrary to the core principles of the agreement. For the WTO and potentially for any FTAA, membership involves the active incorporation into domestic legislation of far-reaching rules that constrain the permissible forms of economic policy and many important aspects of state-society relations. Again, this makes domestic politicization very hard to avoid.

Third, these changes have altered the character of domestic economic coalitions. Within this increasingly intrusive and far-reaching structure of regional or global economic rules, the adoption of particular rules or the exchange of particular negotiating concessions have very clear distributional consequences.[25] It is likely, therefore, that winners and losers will become both more self-aware and better mobilized. And finally, the needs and incentives facing the Brazilian state have changed. On the one hand, the sheer difficulty of calculating the costs and benefits of an agreement across such a wide range of issues (from government procurement to patent protection) means that negotiators need information that only business can provide. On the other, the Brazilian government has, in general, not resisted the involvement of domestic groups and public opinion because that opinion has been mostly supportive of the government's position—with much of it reflecting stronger resistance to the FTAA project. This domestic mobilization may strengthen Brazil's bargaining power or resistance capacity; but it may also complicate the capacity of the Brazilian government to deliver on a final bargain.

Transnational Civil Society

The past decade has seen a great expansion of academic analysis on what has come to be called transnational civil society, both globally and within the Western Hemisphere. Transnational civil society refers to those self-organized intermediary groups that are relatively independent of both public authorities and private economic actors; that are capable of taking collective action in pursuit of their interests or values; and that act across state borders. The roles of such groups within international society have increased very significantly: first, in the formal process of norm creation, standard setting, and norm development; second, in the broader social process by which new norms emerge and find their way on to the international agenda; third, in the detailed functioning of many international institutions and in the processes of implementation and compliance; and fourth, in direct participation in many governance activities (disbursing an increasing proportion of official aid, engaging in large-scale humanitarian relief, and leading efforts at promoting democracy or postconflict social and political reconstruction). In all of these areas the analytical focus has been on transnational networks—for example, knowledge-based networks of economists, lawyers, or scientists; or transnational advocacy networks that act as channels for flows of money and material resources but, more critically, of information, ideas, and values.[26]

Let us first consider the direct role of transnational civil society on the bilateral relationship between the United States and Brazil. It is clear that transnational civil society activity has played an important direct role: the transnational environmental rain forest campaigns of the second half of the 1980s provide the strongest example; mobilization against Brazilian human rights practices by groups such as Amnesty International or Human Rights Watch provide another. It is also clear that such activity is, at a minimum, likely to ensure that the expanded agenda of relations will continue. Whatever governments may decide, political pressure from civil-society groups will ensure that issues such as human rights and the environment remain on the agenda.

And yet it is also the case that the salience and significance of this form of politics varies across time and across issue areas. For example, green activism declined in the United States and Brazil as it did in many parts of the world in the 1990s, and the agendas and priorities of environmental groups shifted. Thus, it may be true in a general sense that what Brazil chooses to do in the Amazon or as regards global warming will profoundly affect the global environment in which we all have to live. And yet, the political salience of environmental issues varies and it is clear that it declined significantly through the 1990s (and in its role as an issue in U.S.-Brazil relations). And, it should be noted that this was the case despite the significant increase in deforestation rates in the Amazon as the Brazilian economy recovered. Changes within transnational civil society have much to do with explaining this variability.

What of the impact of transnational civil society on the regional agenda? Here the impact does appear to have grown over time, as illustrated by the very high levels of mobilization around the FTAA and trade integration. This is a fact of diplomatic life with which all regional foreign ministries now have to contend. Compared to Mexico's, for example, Brazil's engagement with NGOs has become increasingly activist and sophisticated. It has moved a long way from the 1980s, when human rights or environmental NGOs were regularly denounced as subversive.

But this new face of diplomacy represents a particular challenge for Brazil and other Latin American states because transnational civil society does not stand outside of regional power structures.[27] Consider, first of all, state power. State action may by shaped by NGO lobbying, but it is often state action that is crucial in fostering the emergence of civil society in the first place and in providing the institutional framework that enables it to flourish. In some cases the links with states are direct. For example, in their analysis of what they term "insider" networks associated with the FTAA process, Roberto Patricio Koreniewiecz and William C. Smith note, "These 'insider' networks did not emerge spontaneously. On the contrary, the societal actors that created these 'insider' networks were to a great extent able to overcome their collective action problems because of the encouragement and support that many of them have received from state agencies and multilateral financial institutions. It is particularly notable that the U.S. government agencies such as USAID and the NSC were active in encouraging civil society participation in the first summit. The Canadian government has also played a significant funding role in support of collaborative civil society endeavors."[28]

State power is increasingly determined by the ability of governments to work successfully within civil society and to exploit transnational and transgovernmental coalitions for their own purposes. We thus need to note the very different capacity of countries to operate within these arenas. Countries such as the United States accustomed to pluralist politics adapt easily to such changes. Many developing countries have found it much harder to navigate in this kind of world, perhaps due to domestic political sensitivities or to inherited traditions of very statist foreign policy making.

Second, there is the question of power within transnational civil society. There is nothing normatively special or sacred about civil society. It is an arena of politics like any other in which the good and thoroughly awful coexist, in which the pervasive claims made by social movements and NGOs to authenticity and representativeness need to be tested and challenged, and in which outcomes may be just as subject to direct manipulation by powerful actors as in the world of interstate politics. As Laurence Whitehead puts it, "All that need concern us here is the conclusion that, whichever historical route [in the development of civil society] may have been followed, the resulting patterns of associative life and social communication will be highly structured, with insiders, traditionally favoured sectors, and marginal or excluded sectors."[29]

Applied internationally, this insight focuses attention on the links between NGOs and particular parts of the international system. The period since 1990 has seen many calls for greater NGO involvement in regional economic negotiations, often presented as part of an argument for greater transparency and democracy. And yet the problem for countries such as Brazil is that such moves tend to work to favor the values and interests of northern states and societies and to thereby magnify still further the power of the already powerful. As Ngaire Woods points out, the risk is that transnational NGOs add yet another channel of influence to those peoples and governments who are already powerfully represented.[30] For example, of the 738 NGOs that were accredited at the Third Ministerial Conference of the WTO at Seattle, 97 were based in developing countries; that is, about 87 percent came from the industrialized countries. Even in the case of more radical grassroots movements, the issues of asymmetry and of dependence on northern funding sources remain.[31]

Finally, we might note an instance of transnational activity that has been crucial elsewhere in the region but almost totally absent from Brazil: the transnational diffusion of neoliberal economic ideas that was characteristic of Chile in the 1970s and of Argentina and Mexico in the 1980s. As Maria Rita Loureiro and Gilberto Tadeu Lima argue, no single external school of economic thought has achieved predominance in Brazil, and economics and economic debates retained a strongly national orientation.[32] Moreover, despite the many cleavages, a degree of consensus on the role of the state and suspicion of excessive market liberalism remained predominant. As Loureiro and Lima note, "Reasons of a historical kind, associated with the role that the state has always needed to assume in Brazil as the regulator and promoter of economic development, may lie at the root of the lack of faith, shared by practically all the different groups of economists, in the capacity of the market, functioning alone, to produce growth and generate stability."[33]

Brazil and the Global Economy

Globalization dominated a very great deal of analysis in the 1990s of Brazil's changing place in the world. For all the problems of definition, globalization involves the dramatic increase in the density and depth of economic, ecological and societal interdependence, with *density* referring to the increased number, range, and scope of cross-border transactions, and *depth* to the degree to which that interdependence affects, and is affected by, the ways in which societies are organized domestically.

In the early 1990s a great deal of this writing—in both Brazil and beyond—had a strongly liberal flavor. Globalization was transforming the possibilities of national economic management as states faced increasingly powerful pressure toward the convergence of economic policies in order to attract foreign investment and technology and in order to compete in an ever more closely linked and competitive marketplace. In Brazil, this view of a changing global economy and of the "exhaustion" of the previous import substitution industrialization (ISI) model explains a good deal of the shift toward Brazil's new policy of "competitive insertion" in the global economy. For the international financial institutions (IFIs) and for many in the developed world, economic reform reflected a genuine and unforced "Latin American convergence" built around the obvious rationality of macroeconomic stability, privatization, and increased openness. A decade or so on, such liberal accounts of globalization appear increasingly shaky.

In the first place, Brazil provides clear evidence against any straightforward notion of convergence, let alone homogenization. Of course, almost all discussion of globalization recognizes that its impact is highly uneven, as some parts of the world are incorporated into ever denser networks of interdependence while other regions are left on, or beyond, the margins. Equally, almost all writers stress the extent to which globalizing forces may produce fragmentation, reaction, or back-lash. But to think principally in these polar terms of incorporation versus exclusion, or of fusion versus fragmentation, is to obscure what is often most in-teresting—that while powerful systemic pressures exist, both processes of change—and, more important, outcomes—vary enormously. The character and intensity of liberalization pressures depend on geopolitical position, level of de-velopment, size, and state strength. Their impact on a country such as Brazil will obviously be very different from their impact on a country such as Chile. In all cases liberalization pressures come up against powerful inherited domestic struc-tures and historically embedded modes of thought. It is important, then, both to acknowledge and to analyze the systemic pressures that have impacted Brazil but, at the same time, to unpack and deconstruct the complex process of break-down and adaptation that has taken place in that country. The result is that the intuitively powerful idea of homogenization breaks down as it becomes clear that, as in the case of Brazil, outcomes conform neither to anything resembling a simple liberal "model" nor to a simple rejection of that model.

Second, there are certainly high levels of economic interdependence between the United States and Brazil, but it is highly asymmetrical. This asymmetry re-mains fundamental to explaining the character of U.S.-Brazil relations. Brazil certainly matters to the United States—for example, the United States exports more to Brazil than to China, India, or Russia; of the top 500 U.S. corporations, 420 currently operate in Brazil; and the total of U.S. investment in Brazil (around US$ 40 billion and concentrated in the financial and manufacturing sectors) is larger than that in China, India, Russia, or even Mexico. Equally, the United States is economically central to Brazil: as a source of foreign investment; as a market, especially for its manufactured goods (recently the top three Brazilian exports to the United States were aircraft, automobile parts, and shoes); and a source of support during financial crises.

This interdependence creates an enormous scope for common interests and provides major incentives against allowing particular tensions to get out of

control. But, in a world where policy makers do not inhabit a Benthamite universal republic of exchange but are naturally driven by mercantilist logics and
domestic protectionist pressures, it is also this asymmetry that underpins much
of the economic friction that has been such a consistent feature of the relationship since the early 1970s. Thus, we have seen repeated Brazilian complaints
against the high levels of U.S. protectionism against Brazilian products in such
areas as steel, ethanol, sugar, shoes, textiles, orange juice, and meat, and the number of antidumping and countervailing duty actions against Brazil. For the United
States, what happens in Brazil has the capacity to affect both U.S. interests and
the quality and character of life in the United States. But economic interdependence is neither strongly structural nor consistently politically salient as liberal
interdependence writing might suggest. Take, for example, the impact of economic and financial developments in Brazil on the stability of the U.S. and global
financial systems. When in 1998–99 there was very real fear of financial conta-
gion across emerging markets, the United States become closely involved in the
Brazilian crisis. However, as the crisis passed for the financial system and, more
important, for the interests of U.S. banks, the issue slipped off the United States's
agenda. The United States is therefore less constrained than in the case of Mexico
from using the power that derives from this asymmetrical interdependence to
press its economic interests in Brazil.

Third, this pattern of asymmetric interdependence is reinforced by Brazil's
structural vulnerability within the global economy. It is this characteristic that
explains much of the continuity in Brazilian understandings of the country's
place in the world. It is true that Brazil remains a relatively closed economy with
the highest average regional tariff and with exports accounting for less than 10
percent of its GDP. But it is also true that Brazil's economic success following the
Real Plan of 1994 was heavily dependent on increased flows of external finance.
In addition, the new pattern of financial crises that took root in the 1990s (beginning with Mexico in 1994, spreading through Asia and Russia, and then back to
Latin America) made Brazil ever more dependent on maintaining investor confidence and on the willingness of the U.S. government (and the financial
institutions based in Washington, D.C.) to provide crisis support (as happened
with Brazil in 1998–99 and again in August 2002).

This is not the place to debate the merits of the particular economic policy
choices taken during the Cardoso administration.[34] But it is to note the impact of
this situation on Brazil's relations with the United States. It led, for example, to
quite strikingly divergent views over the source of Brazil's economic problems.
For many in the United States, Brazil's economic and financial difficulties were
not the result of neoliberalism, but rather resulted from the very failure of Brazil
to engage seriously with domestic economic reform. For many in Brazil, by contrast, the problem lay with the series of destabilizing external shocks that hit

Latin America in the late 1990s, with the failure of markets to distinguish between different Latin American countries, and with the unwillingness of the United States either to assume a leading role in financial crisis management or to appreciate the increasing need for reform of the international financial institutions and for addressing the dangerous instabilities unleashed by globalization.

Similarly, for many in Brazil the "lesson" of the Argentinian economic crisis that gathered speed after 1999 was not primarily that neoliberal economic reform had failed, but rather that even an obsessively pro-American government failed to secure external help and assistance when times became difficult—what Rubens Barbosa has called the U.S. government's "indifference and coldness in the face of the agonized convulsions in Argentina."[35] As in the 1980s, external financial dependence is widely perceived as having a negative impact on Brazil's bargaining power vis-à-vis the United States. The extent to which Brazil has depended on direct U.S. intervention (as in 1999) or on U.S.-supported IMF assistance (as in August 2002) represents an inevitable constraint on Brazil's bargaining capacity. This inevitability is, of course, balanced by the capacity of Brazil (and of a financial crisis in Brazil) to impose costs on the United States, and only holds up to the point where a government concludes that whatever it does or says, nothing is going to alter market sentiment or secure sustained external support.

It is one of the great paradoxes of modern Latin America that dependency theory flourished at a time when the region was less externally dependent than at any time since 1945—in a period that saw a declining U.S. appetite for coercive intervention, the existence of broad balance of global power, opportunities for coalition building and diversification, acceptance of statist or at least reformist economic ideas, and relatively benign global economic conditions. Dependency theory faded as real and renewed dependence set in in the 1980s and as market liberalism triumphed in policy terms.

And yet there is, in fact, great continuity both in the structures of dependency and in the relevance of these structures for explaining Brazil's international position. Dependency-style analyses contain many well-recognized flaws (neglect of the international political system and, above all, an exaggerated image of external imposition). But dependency theory and neoliberalism do not stand in opposition, nor does Cardoso's own "move to the market" necessarily contradict his own earlier writing on the subject. Indeed, his own analysis of Brazil's changing role in an age of globalization reflected a good deal of Brazilian thinking of the 1990s and illustrates the continuity of his own ideas. First, there is Cardoso's view that the driving force for change in the modern world comes from technologically driven globalization: "Behind these changes [the end of the Cold War, etc.] can be found the true revolution of our century: the marriage of science, technology and freedom; of university, business and public authority. . . . And, moreover, together with the marriage of science, technology and freedom, the great tendency of the modern world is the globalization of the economy."[36] Second, there is his argument that this "technocrat-democratic" revolution is not only uniting the world but also leading to larger and more powerful political entities—hence, regionalization and the need to position Brazil in relation to emerging blocs. And third, there is his conclusion that the "old south" has fragmented and that exclusion and marginalization represents a new and more powerful form of dependency. As Cardoso puts it,

> We are dealing, effectively, with a far more cruel phenomenon [than earlier forms of dependency]: Either the South (or a part of it) enters into the democratic-technological-scientific race, invests heavily in research and development, and supports the transformation into an "information economy", or it will become unimportant, unexploited and unexploitable. The South finds itself under a double threat: apparently incapable of inte- grating itself, seeking its own interests, but equally incapable of avoiding "being integrated" as the servant of the richer economies. Those countries (or parts of them) incapable of repeating the revolution of the contempo- rary world, will end up in the "worst of all possible worlds." They will not be worth the trouble of being exploited and will become irrelevant, without any interest to the developing global economy.[37]

LIMITATIONS AND CAVEATS

Interdependence, institutions, civil society, democracy, and globalization are all central themes in the increasing complexity of U.S.-Brazil relations. However, they do not necessarily bring with them either close relations or an absence of tension. The previous section has deliberately sought to bring out the extent to which the tensions and lack of closeness between Brazil and the United States are rooted in divergent hard interests and in asymmetries of power. It is these struc- turally rooted divergences that are most important in explaining the very significant continuity in U.S.-Brazil relations—a continuity that runs across regime and government change in Brazil, shifts in the dominant economic model, and successive changes in administration in the U.S. government. Theoretically this picture pushes us away from liberalism and toward both neorealism and at least some elements of neodependency theory. But, left on its own, this picture is both too crude and too incomplete. Two crucial limitations or caveats need to be noted and examined.

The first has to do with perceptions. The tone of U.S.-Brazil relations has often seemed worse than the "objective" structure of interests would lead us to expect. Perhaps the best recent example comes with the short-lived government of Fernando Collor de Mello. Here, after all, was a new Brazilian president who was determined to end outstanding conflicts with the United States (over intellectual property, sensitive technologies, arms exports, etc.); to introduce a policy of economic liberalization; and to build a new vision of Brazil's role in the world around a rhetoric of modernization and of "joining the First World." But even before his impeachment it was evident that the expected improvement in relations had failed to materialize. In part this followed from the erratic and (to many in the United States) contradictory character of Brazil's attempts at stabilization. But it also followed from the way in which Collor's initiatives were understood in the United States—most notably in Brazil's correct but hardly fulsome support for the United States in the 1991 war on Iraq and the degree to which this stood in marked contrast to Argentina's strident pro-Americanism.[38]

On some occasions we seem to be dealing with direct misperceptions—a simple failure to understand the calculations of power and interest of the other side. Thus Brazil's (and the region's) expectation of significant economic rewards in return for support for the United States in World War II and the early Cold War period seemed absurd and illogical when viewed from the perspective of those concerned with managing Washington's Cold War foreign policy as a whole. But, far more often and of far greater significance, we are dealing with divergent perceptions: the extent to which understandings of issues diverge and clash due to the very different cultural, ideological, or historical "filters" through which policy makers in both countries interpret the world.

During the Cold War it was, of course, anticommunism and national security that provided the most common means for the United States to make sense of the region and to separate friends from foes—in its most extreme form in Ambassador Richard Patterson's duck test. As late as the 1980s, this kind of perceptual dissonance was an important element in the coolness of U.S. relations with Brazil. Thus, on one side, we see the U.S. administration of Ronald Reagan obsessed with fighting communism and subversion in Central America as part of its Cold War struggle; while on the other side, in Brazil we see a conservative military government that had moved toward de facto nonalignment and that viewed anticommunism as simply less important than issues of debt, trade, and development.

In the 1990s, the most common filter was provided by economic liberalism and by the image of Brazil as a "laggard" in the process of economic reform and modernization. For many in both business and political circles in the United States, successive Brazilian governments were simply obtuse and unwilling to recognize the logic and rationality of the market-liberal policies being pressed by both foreign governments and by the IFIs. Thus the United States believed that Brazil was dragging its feet on economic reform in ways that directly harmed U.S. interests. For example, the United States welcomed Brazilian concessions on intellectual property rights (a new Industrial Property Law was passed in 1997 after a seven-year passage through Congress). But it believed that these did not go far enough, and that U.S. firms suffered from inadequate patent and copyright protection. For many, Brazil's laggard status was to be explained by the continuing power of an obscurantist statist ideology and by rent-seeking interest groups.

The most common (but not uncontested) Brazilian view, by contrast, was that its economic needs did not necessarily mean continued liberalization and that excessive liberalization could be destabilizing; that the protection of its established industries was a coherent and rational objective for any government; that the U.S. aggressive emphasis on liberalizing other people's economies stood in hypocritical contrast to its own continued protectionism; and that the United States suffered from self-interested amnesia given the role that a strong state, high tariffs, and mercantilism had played in its own economic development. There was a consistent—if at times faltering—Brazilian view according to which foreigners do not really understand the complexity of the domestic political and economic situation, they lack respect for Brazil's sovereign rights, and they do not realize that Brazil is big enough and resilient enough to take the pressures coming from outside on its own terms and to adapt in its own way to a changing international context.

From the perspective of the analyst, two things are evident. First, much misunderstanding of Brazil within the United States simply reflects a lack of knowledge about Brazil and an all too common failure to grasp the sheer complexity of the country—as illustrated by simplistic comparisons of Brazil's "failure" with Chile's "success." Brazil is, after all, a country that underwent an extraordinary process of economic development and modernization in the twentieth century, and especially in the period from 1945 to 1980. For all its incompleteness, its distortions, and its inequalities, this transformation was comparable in its rapidity and intensity to that which occurred in Germany and the United States in the course of the second half of the nineteenth century.

Second, the common U.S. view of a Brazilian government trapped between "imperatives" of globalization and reform, on the one hand, and a set of political constituencies that steadfastly refused to adapt, on the other, provides—at best—an incomplete account. It downplays the extent of reform that has taken place; but also implies that, freed from domestic opposition and coalitional politics, Brazil would have moved in a clearly liberal and liberalizing direction. In fact, the process of change is not best understood as a simple struggle between a reforming government and obscurantist opposition, nor between the logical acceptance of the values of the liberal globalized world and old-fashioned third-world nationalism. Rather, what is crucial in the Brazilian case is the combining of old themes and old values with new policy options in the face of new constraints and opportunities.

More recently, it is the war on terrorism that has embedded a perceptual filter of a different kind, and one that carries the potential for an escalation of misperception. At the level of official policy the Brazilian government moved quickly to express its firm solidarity with the United States in the aftermath of the events of September 11, 2001, and to mobilize support within the OAS. But over the succeeding months, it also expressed unhappiness at the excessive militarization of the international agenda to the detriment of other international priorities;[39] it criticized U.S. high-handedness and unilateralism; and Cardoso expressed his frustration at the apparent lack of interest and knowledge of South America. There was much resentment in media commentary in Brazil at what Tony Judt has labeled as U.S. "condescending indifference" to outside opinion.[40] On the other side, popular and political anti-Americanism in Brazil added, for many commentators in the United States, to the sense of Brazil's unreliability and lack of seriousness as a potential partner.[41]

The danger of misperceptions has been increased by the sheer difficulty of making sense of the continued complexity (and possible increased confusion) in Brazil. Politically, Brazil has avoided sudden ruptures and clear transitions in which clear alignments and neat ideological cleavages can be identified. Economically, a Brazil that has moved beyond the neoliberalism of the Washington consensus and that has little option but to deal with the enormous challenges of economic and social inequality is likely to engage in a good deal of experimentation and ad hoc thinking that will be difficult to shoehorn into the neat categories of Right and Left.

Simplifying filters are perhaps inevitable, especially given the range and complexity of U.S. foreign policy, the only intermittent appearance of Brazil as a high-level foreign policy interest in the United States, the absence of sustained media coverage and intellectual engagement with Brazil, and the sheer ignorance about Brazil even in political and policy-making circles. And, of course, misperceptions affect both sides. Thus, in Brazilian commentary on the United States there has been a persistent failure to understand the complexity of U.S. politics and foreign policy that feeds all too readily into an excessively conspiratorial view of U.S. actions (and inactions). Here we might also note the very low level of serious academic interest in the United States inside Brazil—at least measured by the number of academic centers, specialists, and university courses devoted specifically to the United States.[42]

The source of these divergent perceptions may be sought in the psychology of individual policy makers and in certain recurring tendencies visible in the way individuals and groups understand the external world and make foreign policy.[43] But foreign relations are also understood through the prism of history and through the mutual images that have been created and reinforced over time, and then institutionalized within dominant foreign policy ideologies. They are therefore related to how actors interpret the world and how their understandings of "where they belong" are formed and institutionally embedded. It may be true (as with the power/interest perspective developed in the first section of this chapter) that all states and all political actors seek power and promote their self-interest. But the crucial question is always, What sorts of power and in pursuit of what kinds of self-interest?[44] Answering such questions takes us into the ways in which both interests and identities are shaped by particular histories and cultures, by domestic factors, and by ongoing processes of interaction with other states.

On the Brazilian side, three features need to be stressed, two of which are central to the continuity of tension, while the third helps us to understand why confrontation has not been more serious.

The first factor concerns the ideology of national autonomy and development. Without trying to make everything fit within a single mold, it is possible to iden-tify an orthodox framework for understanding the history of Brazil's place in the world that unites many foreign policy makers, historians, and analysts. It takes the project of national developmentalism as its central organizing idea. It lays great emphasis on the period from 1930 and, more particularly, from 1945, by which time the economic foundations of the project appear more clearly and are more firmly embedded in economic policy. It places great emphasis on external struc-tures—both the capitalist world economy, which contains far more snares and constraints than opportunities, and the international political system in which the hegemony of the United States is viewed as a natural obstacle to the achievement of Brazilian development and to its upward mobility in the international power hierarchy. Perhaps above all, this way of thinking takes utterly for granted the intrinsic value of national autonomy, of defending economic and political sover-eignty, and of developing a more prominent international role for the country.

Clearly this set of ideas is closely related to the development model of the ISI period and to the autonomy- and development-focused foreign policy that was most visible and influential in the 1970s. But it cannot be reduced to a particular version of national developmentalism. It has continued to influence many of the unspoken assumptions that characterize Brazilian debates on both globalization and U.S. hegemony. Theoretically it draws both on traditional power-political realism (the world as a mean and anarchical place) and on dependency theory and Marxism. Niccolò Machiavelli and Karl Marx are to be found in constant, if not always very consistent, conversation. And, partially in consequence, it draws together both the Right and the Left. This was true in the past (remember just how briefly Brazilian foreign policy was dominated by anticommunism even under military governments, and how much substantive overlap there was between nationalists within the military, on the one hand, and politicians and commentators inspired by dependency theory, on the other.

The second factor concerns the legacy of the Cold War. The most important impact of the Cold War on Brazil was not directly in terms of its international re-lations and foreign policy; rather, it was in terms of the internalization of a particular set of ideological conflicts into domestic politics and the crystallization of a particular image of the United States. It was here that the "overlay" of the Cold War was most powerful; and it is here that powerful, and often negative, images of the United States were created and consolidated. Although popular anti-Americanism has been less virulent than in, say, Argentina, continued (or reawakened) suspicion of a hegemonic United States owes much to the legacy of U.S. Cold War actions and policies; and to the way in which these actions and policies formed part of the reality of domestic Brazilian politics. They were not just something in the world "out there," but impacted on how domestic politics was practiced and experienced.

It is also relevant to note the absence in the post-1945 period of the idea of a special relationship as a major theme in the foreign policies of either the United States or Brazil. It is true that the logic of developing close relations with major regional powers ("regional influentials," "pivotal regional players") has been a theme of U.S. foreign policy that appears intermittently. Its most sustained manifestation was in the early 1970s with the Nixon Doctrine and with the importance that Secretary of State Henry Kissinger placed on Brazil in the context of a changing global agenda. But it has remained only a marginal policy option. For a long period there was concern in the United States that too strong a pro-Brazil policy would only complicate U.S. relations with the rest of the region. More important, the pull of solid U.S. interests has simply not appeared strong enough; as we have seen, there have been persistent doubts as to Brazil's reliability and openness to cooperative relations; and the United States has believed that it could get what it wanted from Brazil (market opening, intellectual property laws) through a mixture of pressure and relatively low-level engagement. On the Brazilian side, although "bandwagoning" with the United States has been a theme in Brazilian policy thinking (in the 1940s, immediately after 1964, and very briefly under Collor), it has generally been viewed as too constraining; the likely benefits were not viewed as large enough to compensate for the restrictions on policy autonomy; and there have been persistent concerns over the lack of constancy and consistency in U.S. support for countries in a region that (apart from Mexico) has remained of secondary importance in U.S. policy.

Yet if these two factors help explain the continuity of strained relations, the third factor pushes in the opposite direction. This concerns Brazil as a "power-maximizing" state. At first blush it seems obvious that Brazil has been concerned with increasing its power and influence and that this power maximization was bound to lead to clashes and tensions with the United States. After all, predictions that Brazil was destined to play a more influential role in world affairs have a long history inside Brazil and have been a theme of much outside commentary. Their intensity has varied across time. At times ideas about greatness have often been no more than a vague aspiration, and not tied to "practical political action."[45] At other times they have assumed a much more direct role in the shaping of foreign policy, as in the 1970s, when the high growth rates of the so-called economic miracle seemed to establish the country as an upwardly mobile middle power, if not one moving ineluctably toward eventual great power status. And, as discussed above, they form one important element in the ideology of developmentalism.

And yet, Brazil has not played the power-political game in the way that either the rhetoric of its leaders or realist theory would lead us to expect. There have been many occasions when power resources have not been developed or exploited and a persistent tendency to downplay hard, especially militarized, power projection. There has often appeared to be a significant gap between recurring intimations of influence and the low-key, risk-averse, and sometimes diffident policies followed in practice, as well as by the generally low priority accorded to foreign policy. Brazil is neither an unconditional status quo power nor a deeply revisionist state. It has no really serious grievances, nor is it completely satisfied. Many of its goals are defensive and continue to reflect its economic interests and its continued economic vulnerability. Others involve a more direct effort to increase its international influence. Thus, although power has mattered for Brazilian policy makers and continues to do so, a simple power-maximization model does not fit the Brazilian case. The point here is that, if we think counterfactually, we can easily imagine a path leading to much greater conflict and tension with the United States. Had Brazil been a more straightforwardly power-maximizing state and had it developed a hard rather than soft revisionist foreign policy, then the relationship with the United States would have been far more prone to conflict and tension.

Brazil, then, does not fit the ideal types of "power state," "trading state," or "revisionist state." There can be no simple explanation for this, but much has to do with the character of state formation and with Brazil's geopolitical location. As Latin American states were formed in the course of the nineteenth century they were generally able to escape the destructive dynamic between state making and war making that was such a feature of the European Westphalian order. Brazil secured its (usually very remote) frontiers with its neighbors in the late nineteenth and early twentieth centuries on successful terms and mostly peacefully. In territorial terms it became a status quo power. With the exception of relations with Argentina, it continued to avoid serious security dilemmas with its neighbors. This left it free to develop an ideology and practice of modernization and national development that was largely inner-directed, responding to domestic failures and aimed at integrating national territory, at upholding domestic order, and at promoting economic development.[46]

What of the United States? U.S. foreign policy has always involved a complex interplay of different foreign policy traditions, and the analysis of U.S. foreign policy is hardly susceptible to easy generalization. But there are two features that have been consistently important in relations with Brazil, generating both misperceptions and recurrent frustrations. First, the United States has rarely framed its foreign policy in a realist language of hard power and interest, but instead within an ideology of values and justice that reflects its own historical values and traditions. Kissingerian realism remains the outlier and the exception. Moreover, this intertwining of interests and values has united liberal and conservative traditions of U.S. foreign policy. The complex links between hard interests and moral values has often impeded successful bargaining and reinforced Brazilian suspicions of the true intentions of the United States. Second, the United States has rarely viewed the Americas as simply a collection of states like any other in which conflicting power and interests are to be managed, mediated, and negotiated. One of the great differences between the informal British empire in the region in the nineteenth century and contemporary U.S. hegemony concerns the scope of concern. Although hard interests may have dominated U.S. policy (keeping out geopolitical rivals and promoting hard economic interests), the United States has consistently involved itself in a broader set of goals concerning how other societies are to be organized and what regional values should be promoted. And, for all the vagueness of the formulation, "hegemonic presumption" remains—the idea that the United States is the natural leader within its own backyard with special rights and an expectation that regional states will fall into line. Deference is to be expected rather than earned and rewarded.

IMPLICATIONS AND PROSPECTS

How much has the election of President Lula altered this inherited picture? What is the impact of the dramatic changes that have taken place in U.S. foreign and security policy as the conflicts over terrorism and Iraq have intensified?

The first statements and early actions of Brazil's foreign policy under Lula suggest very significant continuities. Several of the trends that were visible in the latter part of the Cardoso administration have been strengthened, and there is very little sign of any major rupture in either the broad pattern of Brazilian foreign policy or in relations with the United States. Moreover, most commentary on the early months of the Lula government has stressed the moderation of policy choices and policy implementation, including those directed toward the United States. And yet, there have been important differences of emphasis within this broad continuity and, of course, relations have been evolving within a dramatically evolving global context.

Let us look first at the overall direction and tenor of foreign policy. As with all governments since 1930 (with the partial exception of the first post-1964 military government) the Lula administration has stressed the very close links between foreign policy and development policy. This can be seen in two areas. In the first place, it is visible in the renewed drive to expand export markets and to diversify Brazil's foreign economic relations. Within this recurrent theme, there has been a much more pronounced emphasis on expanding relations with other major developing countries (especially China, India, and South Africa) and a return of significant elements of Brazil's earlier third-world policy, both in terms of the language of foreign policy and in policy itself (especially toward Africa). Second, the links between foreign and economic policy are clearly visible in the need to project an image of moderation and to reassure international markets. Brazil remains externally vulnerable in the face of a continuing decline in foreign investment flows, high interest rates, the absence of economic recovery in the United States, and the potential economic damage to the global economy posed by conflict in the Middle East. Thus, the incoming Brazilian government has been very concerned with projecting a moderate image, both to reassure markets in the face of its continued financial vulnerability, but also to undercut conservative commentators in the United States who claim to see a new "axis of evil" in South America made up of allegedly nationalist and radical leaders including Fidel Castro, Chávez, and Lula.

There is also broad continuity in Brazil's generally negative view of the international economic and political system: the malfunctioning of the global financial system; the continued protectionism in the developed world and the broken trade promises; the distortion of the global agenda with the militarization of the so-called war against terrorism pushing aside more fundamental issues and problems; the extent to which multilateralism is under severe challenge, in terms of both the difficulties facing the Doha Trade Round and the crisis within the UN as a result of the Iraq conflict. Although picking up on themes that were visible under Cardoso, Brazil's language on many of these issues has hardened and, more important, there is a clear determination to project a concern for social justice as the international counterpart of Lula's domestic agenda. This concern with justice issues was visible in Lula's speeches in both Davos and at the NGO Global Forum in Porto Alegre. Thus, to take one example, Lula has stressed that "alongside the theme of security, the international agenda should also privilege those issues that aim at the eradication of asymmetries and injustices, such as the struggle against social and cultural exclusion, the genuine opening of the markets of the rich countries, the construction of a new financial architecture, and the imperative of combating hunger, disease, and poverty."[47]

How much this broad foreign policy orientation directly impacts relations with the United States is unclear. Brazil, as with all middle powers, has a natural and major national interest in the sustainability of multilateral institutions for the reasons outlined earlier in this chapter. To the extent that hard-line unilateralism prevails in the United States, this is likely to be an ongoing source of divergence. Equally, Brazil has sought to find common cause with other major developing countries in trade and other negotiations, and this harder line is likely to continue. (Yet it is of course aimed not just at the United States but also at Europe—where the differences are very serious particularly given the impact of EU agricultural policy and the deep tension in Pascal Lamy's (trade commissioner of the EU, 1999–2004) support for a "development round," on the one hand, and, on the other, his inability to move on agriculture.

Second, there is the foreign policy-making process. The Lula administration has placed great emphasis on the need to open up foreign policy to a wider range of domestic voices and interests. The government has declared its intent on involving, in particular, civil society groups and NGOs to a greater extent than under the previous government, and particularly on such issues as the FTAA and human rights. It remains to be seen exactly how much of a change this will involve, but there are two areas with the potential to destabilize relations with the United States. The first concerns the FTAA, to which there has been considerable grassroots opposition (including within and around the Workers Party), and where greater domestic involvement may well make negotiations more politicized and any final bargain harder to strike and sell. The second concerns giving greater voice to anti-Americanism more generally, especially in the light of the war against Iraq (see below).

Third, the Lula government has given very high priority to South America, and especially to MERCOSUR. Again much of this follows the pattern of the 1990s when MERCOSUR was seen not as a policy but as part of Brazil's "destiny." As the chapters in this volume have stressed, and as spokespeople for the new administration have noted, MERCOSUR plays a strategic role in Brazilian foreign policy, in at least four ways: (1) as part of a national economic project of using economic subregionalism as a means of controlled integration into a globalizing world and as offering at least a small degree of protection against external shocks and vulnerabilities; (2) as a platform for securing a greater regionalist voice for Brazil in South America; (3) as the political framework for managing both interstate and intersocietal relations with the countries of the MERCOSUR area and the interdependencies that have emerged from the previous successes of MERCOSUR; and (4) as part of its externally focused political strategy of increasing its leverage and bargaining power, both in multilateral forums and in crucial external relationships, above all in relation to the EU and the United States. The new administration has invested a good deal of rhetorical energy and high-level time and effort in seeking to relaunch MERCOSUR; in locating some basis for the restoration of economic ties that have fallen apart so badly in the face of the Argentinian crisis; in seeking new areas for cooperation, such as in the social field; and in indicating a greater willingness to bear costs and make some concessions in order to help sustain the regionalist project. MERCOSUR's role within the broader pattern of Brazilian thinking toward the United States has thus not been radically altered. Indeed, in many ways the dominant trend of the 1990s has been strengthened.

Where there has been greater change is in Brazil's relations with other parts of the region and in the new government's declared aim of playing a more active and activist political role. This has been most noticeable in relation to the crises in Venezuela and Colombia. Brazil has sought to play a more active role in the Venezuelan crisis as one of the Group of Friends—and indeed, in establishing the group in the first place and in the debates over its membership. In the case of Colombia, there has been both greater awareness of the serious dangers posed to Brazil by spillovers from the Colombian conflict: increasing incidents on the border, environmental impacts, drug violence and criminality, increased impact of the drug trade inside Brazil. This has not simply increased insecurity in the border areas but has been linked with the deterioration of societal insecurity and increased social and criminal violence inside Brazil. What appears to be novel is the declared willingness of the new Brazilian government to play a political role in Colombia or, at least, to declare that it has a major political interest in the conflict.

There is no reason why this should necessarily involve tension with the United States. A Brazil with a clearly defined set of regional goals and with a shared interest in managing destabilizing regional crises is indeed a potentially valuable partner for the United States—and has been seen as such. And there is a clear shared interest in the problem of uncontrolled areas ("ungoverned spaces," as one leading U.S. military figure has labeled them) where both drug and terrorist activity is able to flourish. Yet, equally, there is considerable scope for misperception and divergence. U.S. and Brazilian government readings of the situation in both Colombia and Venezuela vary quite markedly. Brazil remains highly resistant to any increased "militarization" of the Colombian conflict and suspicious of U.S. intentions toward Chávez in Venezuela. The government of Brazil maintains its stand against any formalized regional security cooperation. And the still very limited military capabilities of Brazil and still ambiguous and ambivalent character of Brazilian ambitions at regional leadership work against the United States coming to view Brazil as a "regional manager" in some kind of sustainable shared partnership.

Fourth, there is the regional economic agenda and the FTAA. Here it is clear that the "shadow boxing" of the 1990s and the dominance of technical discussions are giving way to serious political engagement and to a period of increasingly hard political bargaining. At the Quito Ministerial Meeting of the FTAA in 2002 the United States and Brazil took over the joint chairmanship of the process. Despite the antagonism of many within the Brazilian Workers Party to the FTAA, the Lula government quickly made it clear that it would engage seriously in the final phase of FTAA negotiations. The general determination to press hard for Brazilian interests remained, but with a declared difference, namely, that the hard issues should be faced early and directly rather than left to a later decision to approve or not the final text of an FTAA agreement.

And yet, the differences remain serious and stark. For the United States the FTAA is not just about trade, but about cementing a wide set of rules and disciplines that will shape Latin American markets in ways that promote U.S. interests. These cover intellectual property, investment protection, government procurement, and services as well as the broader convergence of standards around U.S. models. It also provides a favorable forum to secure the management of such issues as environment or labor standards. And it also remains an important instrument in its broader trade strategy, with the USTR playing multilateralism, regionalism, and bilateralism against each other in a game of "competitive liberalization" in order to maximize U.S. bargaining influence. For Brazil the great dilemma is that the United States shows little sign of being willing to remove or reduce the protectionist instruments that it has used to restrict Brazilian manufactured exports (especially antidumping and countervailing duties); and even less willingness to negotiate on agriculture outside of the WTO. Moreover, domestic protectionist pressures restrict the effective margin of maneuver of all U.S. administrations. The strength of such pressures could be seen in the narrow passage of the TPA and in the cases of increased farm support and steel tariffs.

Finally, there is the impact of the so-called war on terrorism and of the U.S.-led military campaign against Iraq. This is an issue over which there are certainly some common interests, at least in terms of a shared recognition of the general danger posed to international society by terrorist groups. But it is also an area where there are divergent concrete interests and, far more important, one that has the potential to exacerbate the two countries' divergent perceptions of each other and of the broader global context within which their relations are embedded. In this respect it illustrates very clearly the broader pattern delineated in this chapter. Divergent interests exist in three areas. First, there is divergence in terms of the relative priority attached to this aspect of security. Terrorism is a serious and generalized threat, but its salience for individual states varies widely. Brazil's security agenda is likely to continue to be dominated by societal insecurity, domestic social violence, and spillovers from neighboring states. Insofar as the United States views regional conflicts through the lens of antiterrorism (as in Colombia) or lays primary emphasis on the need to counter regionalist terrorist threats (including Washington's concern over the activities of Hezbollah in the triborder area of South America where Brazil, Argentina, and Paraguay meet), then friction is likely to result. Second, there is divergence in terms of understanding the sources of global insecurity. Although polls indicate that terrorism and weapons proliferation are viewed as threats by many Brazilians, many see the rich/poor gap and the threat of acquired immune deficiency syndrome (AIDS) as equally important dangers to the world.[48] Third, there is divergence in terms of the negative impact that the confrontation against Iraq has had on global institutions. Brazil has a very strong interest in the maintenance of multilateralism and is bound to see the damage inflicted on the UN as a result of the as a threat to its own interests—however much the issue may be presented in the language of law and morality.

More important, however, is the divergence in perceptions and the very different views of the world that the war on terrorism and the confrontations in the
Middle East have reinforced. In the United States, not only has hegemonic re-
assertionism remained popular but so too has the belief that U.S. actions serve
not only its own interests but also those of the broader international community.
In Brazil, by contrast (and this is true in many other parts of both Latin America
and the developing world), there has been a very powerful perception that the
war against Iraq formed part of a much broader and self-interested neoimperial
project that will inevitably work to limit and constrain the freedom and autonomy of even relatively well-positioned middle powers that reflect divergent
social and political values.

This combination of divergent interests and dissonant perceptions highlights
the difficulty of finding a stable basis for accommodation and for a sustainable
cooperative basis for managing relations. Certainly the early months of 2003 saw a
sharpening of the dilemma of how to live with a United States whose huge hegemonic power appears to have been galvanized by a much clearer hegemonic project
and sense of purpose. As Lula's foreign policy adviser put it in a recent interview,
"The economic, political and military weight of the United States is so gigantic that
those who do not accept it are placed in the following position: either they submit
or they remain in a position of virtual confrontation with the United States."[49]

What does this mean for the future of U.S.-Brazil relations? It is certainly possible to imagine a scenario in which the logic of improving relations with the
United States, even of considering the possibility of "bandwagoning" and alignment increases very significantly—a hemisphere consolidating strongly under
clear U.S. hegemonic leadership and witnessing sustained and successful regional
political and economic integration; and a world in which Europe is internally
deeply divided; in which multilateralism has been significantly eroded; and in
which the global economy continues to stall. If the hemisphere were to close in
this way (as happened in the immediate post-1945 period), then Brazil's options
would be narrow indeed. However, not only does such a scenario face major limits (not least because of very clear global engagement on the part of the United
States), but any move toward close alignment with the United States goes against
the whole tenor of inherited Brazilian thinking on foreign policy and against a
great deal of Brazilian domestic opinion. Here we might note the impact of domestic constraints on Mexico's freedom to align with the United States in the war
on Iraq, despite the massive incentives facing the Mexican government and the
much higher levels of pro-American feeling in Mexico compared to Brazil.

The more likely scenario is a continuation of the inherited pattern of relatively low-level friction, unmet expectations, and recurrent frustration. On the
one hand, divergence over concrete issues is likely to continue (as with differences over market access and agriculture in relation to the FTAA), while the Iraq

conflict and the struggle against terrorism is likely to continue to generate very different views of world politics. On the other hand, there will remain great awareness of the costs of overt conflict with the United States and there are other issues on which perceptions of common interest could increase (as with the need for cooperation to combat the drug trade and money laundering).

The centrality of U.S. power means that it will be the balance of arguments within the U.S. administration and Congress that will prove decisive. In terms of U.S. regional policy, a number of factors point toward Brazil becoming significantly more central, and toward a more sustained level of salience and engagement. The FTAA is the most significant issue on the Bush administration's regional agenda, and Brazil remains central to a successful outcome to the FTAA—despite the tactic of putting pressure on Brazil by threatening to negotiate bilaterally or with smaller regional groupings. Brazil also becomes more important as relations with Mexico have deteriorated after the events of September 11, 2001, and as other parts of the region seem ever more crisis prone. Even for those for whom South America is wholly marginal and irrelevant, a deteriorating regional situation could become a real distraction from the task of dealing with terrorism and rogue states. A worsening regional situation would also impact negatively on hard U.S. security interests in the region, especially in Colombia; and perhaps also spill over and affect Mexico. On the other hand, a good deal of U.S. Latin American policy continues to be run by those for whom an older mind-set is still dominant and for whom Colombia, Cuba, and Venezuela are likely to remain the dominant priorities.

Perhaps more than anywhere else in the hemisphere, the future of U.S.-Brazil relations will depend on the broader policy battles that are being, and will be, fought out in the U.S. government. Brazil is very unlikely to be viewed as particularly important by those who argue that the sheer hegemonic dominance of the United States renders unipolarity stable; that the best strategy is to maximize U.S. military and coercive power and its freedom for maneuvering by avoiding binding treaties and messy involvement in institutions and periphery issues; and that the United States should not be afraid to use its power actively to organize the world in a way that forestalls and preempts threats. Brazil (and countries like it) will become more important only when and if opinion and influence shifts toward those who hold a different view of U.S. foreign policy—those who stress the complexity of both U.S. power and interests; who argue that the United States needs both allies and institutions if the problems of a globalized world are to be managed effectively; and who doubt that a sustainable and legitimate order can be based solely, or even primarily, on hierarchy, coercion, and imposition. How this debate is played out, both globally and in terms of U.S. policy toward the Western Hemisphere, will be the most decisive factor influencing the future character of U.S.-Brazil relations.

NOTES FOR CHAPTER I

1. In the Americas, Brazil's territorial size stands third after Canada and the United States, while its population and economy (gross domestic product) stands second, after the United States.

2. Bradford Burns, *The Unwritten Alliance: Rio Branco and the Brazilian-American Relations* (New York: Columbia University Press, 1966).

3. Despite vigorous U.S. protectionism at this time, Brazil was assured tariff exemptions or reductions for many of its U.S.-bound products, particularly coffee. In turn, Brazil reciprocated by lowering its tariffs on U.S. products by a range of 20 to 30 percent.

4. Between the years 1914 and 1928, U.S. participation in Brazilian imports grew from 14 to 26 percent. The goods destined for Brazil included automobiles and accessories, wheat, gas, steam engines, cement, and electronic machines and appliances.

5. Gerson Moura, *Autonomia na Dependência. A Política Externa Brasileira de 1935 à 1942* (Rio de Janeiro: Nova Fronteira, 1980).

6. Mônica A. Hirst, "Era Vargas," in *História das Relações Internacionais do Brasil*, ed. Raul Mendes Silva and Clóvis Brigagão (Rio de Janeiro: CEBRI/Petrobrás, 2001).

7. Under this provision of the Trade Act of 1974, as amended, the president is required to take all appropriate action, including retaliation, to obtain the removal of any act, policy, or practice of a foreign government that violates an international agreement or is unjustifiable, unreasonable, or discriminatory, and burdens or restricts U.S. commerce. In practice, this provision has been employed increasingly on behalf of American exporters fighting foreign import barriers or subsidized competition in foreign markets.

1. Former U.S. ambassador to Brazil (1999–2001) Anthony Harrington's statement was a recent example of such complaints. While mentioning a list of expectations vis-à-vis Brazil at a conference at the American Chamber of Commerce, his words were clear: "Unpredictability make our investors nervous." Jose Meirelles Passos, "Amigo de Clinton diz que corrupcão no Brasil é um problema persistente," *O Globo*, November 4, 1999.

2. Inflation rates declined from a monthly average of 40 percent in early 1994 to an annual rate of 22 percent in 1995, 9.34 percent in 1996, 7.48 percent in 1997, and 0.71 percent in 1998.

3. The financial assistance package for Brazil involved $18 billion from the International Monetary Fund, $4.5 billion from both the World Bank and the Inter-American Development Bank, and bilateral credit, $5 billion of which was provided by the U.S. and $9.5 billion by European governments. See Eliana Cardoso, "Brazil's Currency Crisis: The Shift from an Exchange Rate Anchor to a Flexible Regime," in *Exchange Rate Politics in Latin America*, ed. Carol Wise and Riordan Roett (Washington, D.C.: Brookings Institution Press, 2000), 85.

4. Between January and March the value of the *real* against the dollar reached 2.2; by early May it settled at 1.68.

5. Gross domestic product growth rates were 2.8 percent in 1996, 3.2 percent in 1997, and 0.5 percent in 1998.

6. In 1999 the most important U.S. multinationals exporters to Brazil were General Motors, Motorola, Lucent, Ford, Du Pont, Compaq, Monsanto, and Caterpillar.

7. "U.S. Barriers on Brazilian Goods and Services," report prepared by the Brazilian Embassy in Washington D.C., November, 2000; www.brazilemb.org.

8. In February 2000 new duties were imposed on U.S. steel imports that affected Brazil as well as the European Union, Japan, and the Ukraine.

9. Antidumping duties were imposed in the United States on cold-rolled steel imports from six countries: Argentina, Brazil, Japan, Russia, South Africa, and Thailand.

10. Robert Guy Matthews, "Steel Union Seeks Changes in Pacts," *Wall Street Journal*, September 19, 2001.

11. See World Trade Organization, *Trade Policy Review*, Brazil 1996, vol. 1, 33–34.

12. This was the case of quotas imposed by the Brazilian government on automobiles; it was withdrawn after the WTO Balance of Payments Committee rejected Brazil's justification. The United States was among the countries to complain against Brazil's new quota regime.

13. See chapter 1, note 7.

14. The previous round, named the Uruguay Round, took place during the years 1986–94.

15. According to WTO norms, all 142 member states ought to agree to the contents of the declaration for its approval.

16. See Pedro da Motta Veiga, "El MERCOSUR y el Proceso de la Construcción de ALCA," in *Integración y Comércio* (Buenos Aires: INTAL, 1998), 3–32; Maria Regina Soares de Lima, "Brazil's Response to the New Regionalism," in *Foreign Policy and Regionalism in the Americas*, ed. Gordon Mace and Jean-Pierre Thérien (Boulder, Colo.: Lynne Rienner, 1996), 137–58.

17. See Mônica Hirst, "Democracia, Seguridad e Integracion," in *America Latina en un Mundo en Transicion* (Buenos Aires: Ediciones Norma, 1996), 189–222.

18. See Richard Feinberg, *Summitry of the Americas: A Progress Report* (Washington, D.C.: Institute for International Economics, 1997).

19. See Riordan Roett, ed., *MERCOSUR: Regional Integration, World Markets* (Boulder, Colo.: Lynne Rienner, 1999), 113.

20. Ibid., 115.

21. Three meetings took place in Brazil: the first in Florianópolis (September 1996), the second in Rio de Janeiro (April 1997), and the third in Belo Horizonte (May 1997). See Motta Veiga, 1998.

22. These were the words of President Cardoso at the meeting. See "ALCA não é um destino inevitável," *O Estado de Sao Paulo*, April 23, 2001.

23. "The bill, known as "fast-track" negotiating authority, would allow Mr. Bush to negotiate trade deals and bring them back to Congress for an expedited, up-or-down vote. No amendments would be allowed.

The legislation was in place in the early 1970s but expired in 1994. Its renewal in the House has been mired in partisan disagreement over whether trade agreements should promote labor and environmental standards, a major issue for Democrats, and how to promote a strong congressional role in trade policy.

The bill that passed yesterday did not address the issue fully enough for most Democrats, who voted 189-21 against the bill. But 194 Republicans backed the legislation, with 23 opposed. Two independents joined in the opposition." Carter Dougherty, "House Approves Fast-Track Measure," *Washington Times*, December 7, 2001.

24. Carla Hills was U.S. trade representative in the years 1989–93 and is currently chair and chief executive of Hills and Company, a consulting firm based in Washington, D.C. See Carla Hills, "Por que precisamos de um acordo de livre comércio para as América," *Politica Externa* 10, no. 2 (2001): 27.

NOTES FOR CHAPTER 3

1. See Deborah Norden and Roberto Russell, *The United States and Argentina: Changing Relations in a Changing World* (New York: Routledge, 2002).

2. Michael Mastanduno, "Preserving the Unipolar Moment: Realist Theories and the U.S. Grand Strategy after the Cold War," in *Unipolar Politics*, ed. Ethan Kapstein and Michael Mastanduno (New York: Columbia University Press, 1999), 199.

3. In the years 1995–2001 President Cardoso met President Clinton five times and President Bush two times. For more details, see the chronology of events at the end of chapter 1.

4. The meeting took place in the United States on November 8, 2001.

5. United Nations, *Statistical Yearbook, Forty-Fifth Issue* (UN, 2000).

6. The world satellite-launching industry is expected to grow by 20 percent each year. With the capacity for fourteen launchings a year, the Alcantara base in Brazil could bring the country an estimated $30 million annually. Simon Romero, "Brazil Is Allowing U.S. Companies to Use Launching Site," *New York Times*, April 19, 2000.

7. Such a perception was mentioned in interviews the author conducted with Brazilian government officials in 1999–2000.

8. Regarding the political crisis in Paraguay, a description of earlier coordination between the United States and Brazil appears in Arturo Valenzuela, *Lessons from the Paraguayan Crisis of 1996. A Report to the Carnegie Commission on Preventing Deadly Conflict* (New York: Carnegie Commission, 1999), 32.

9. See Monica Herz and João Nogueira, *Ecuador vs. Peru* (Boulder, Colo.: Lynne Rienner, 2002), 49–96.

10. Jennifer Rich, "World Business Briefing: America's Brazil Decision Benefits Postponed," *New York Times*, August 3, 2000.

11. Larry Rother, "Brazil Begins to Take Role on the World Stage," *New York Times*, August 30, 2000.

12. Ibid.

13. Richard Feinberg, *Summitry of the Americas: A Progress Report* (Washington, D.C.: Institute for International Economics, 1997), 195, and Riordan Roett, "U.S. Policy toward MERCOSUR: From Miami to Santiago," in *MERCOSUR: Regional Integration, World Markets*, ed. Riordan Roett (Boulder, Colo.: Lynne Rienner, 1999), 113–15. See also Sidney Weintraub, *Development and Democracy in the Southern Cone* (Washington, D.C.: CSIS Press, 2000).

14. The conference took place in Brasilia, November 22–24, 2000.

15. In August 2000 President Bill Clinton traveled to Colombia to announce the Colombia Plan, which involved a $1.3 billion aid package and to reaffirm full support for the government of Andres Pastrana. Eighty percent of the aid package was for military use, which involves the formation of three 1,000-men antidrug battalions, 500 military advisers, and 60 helicopters.

16. When referring to Plan Colombia at a joint news conference with Secretary of State Madeleine K. Albright, Brazilian Foreign Minister Luiz Felipe Lampreia stated, "We do not have the same degree of commitment. . . . We have no intention of participating in any common or concerted international action." Rother, "Brazil Begins to Take Role on the World Stage."

17. Weintraub, *Development and Democracy in the Southern Cone*, 67.

18. This treaty was signed by both countries during Clinton's 1997 visit to Brazil. Though the U.S. Senate approved the treaty in October 1998, in 2000 it still awaited Brazilian congressional approval.

19. *International Narcotics Control Strategy Report* (Washington, D.C.: Government Printing Office,: 2000), 1–2.

20. The Educational Program for Resistance to Drugs and Violence deserves a special mention for the training of uniformed state military police drug education volunteers in seventeen of Brazil's twenty-six states.

21. Interagency coordination led by the Antidrug Secretariat became a source of political problems since the creation of the secretariat (1998) as competition between military and police authority in border control operations became explicit. The secretariat was perceived as enhancing military presence in drug combat and prevention policies due to both its initial command by a retired military officer and its subordination to the presidency via the military. The presence of the military in the suppression of drug trafficking was strengthened by the 1998 legislation authorizing the military to interdict civilian aircraft—by force if necessary. This new prerogative has been indirectly connected with the enforcement of a militarily controlled Amazon Surveillance System. According to the Ministry of Justice, the new secretariat should restrict its actions to training and educational activities. In 2000 the escalation of interbureaucratic conflicts led to the complete renewal of authorities and redefinition of responsibilities in counternarcotics activities. Ever since the secretariat was put in charge of training and educational programs, the federal police, subordinate to the Ministry of Justice, assumed full responsibility for repressive actions.

22. The U.S. government has become especially interested in the approval of an omnibus counternarcotics bill that was sent to Congress in 1996.

23. Transnational advocacy networks are characterized by voluntary, reciprocal, and horizontal exchanges of information and services. See Margaret E. Keck and Kathryn Sikkink, *Activists beyond Borders* (Ithaca, N.Y.: Cornell University Press, 1998), 8.

24. In the United States, the main organizations were the Washington Office on Latin America and the Council on Hemispheric Affairs.

25. Edward Cleary, *The Struggle for Human Rights in Latin America* (Westport, Conn.: Praeger, 1997), 141–43.

26. For a general comparison between repressive political apparatus in the Southern Cone and Brazil in the 1970s see Carlos Acuña and Catalina Smulovitz, "Adjusting the Armed Forces to Democracy: Successes, Failures and Ambiguities in the Southern Cone," in *Constructing Democracy: Successes, Failures and Ambiguities in the Southern Cone*, eds. Elizabeth Jelin and Charles Hershberg (Boulder, Colo.: Westview, 1993).

27. A clear sign of this sort of change was the cable sent in 1979 by Amnesty International to President João Figueiredo in Brazil acknowledging the amnesty as a "positive step towards a return to the rule of law in Brazil." *Amnesty International Report 1980* (London: Amnesty International Publications, 1980), 113.

28. Both the UN Human Rights Commission and the Inter-American Court of Human Rights at the OAS began making extensive use of NGO information.

29. Keck and Sikkink, *Activists beyond Borders*, 68.

30. The most important organizations are Amnesty International, Human Rights Watch, the Lawyers Committee on Human Rights, the Washington Office on Latin America, and the American Anthropological Association.

31. In 1982, the National Human Rights Movement was created. In 1991, 223 human rights centers functioned all over the country.

32. *Police Abuse in Brazil: Summary Executions and Torture in Sao Paulo and Rio de Janeiro* (New York: Americas Watch, 1987), 26.

33. Keck and Sikkink, *Activists beyond Borders*, 69.

34. Cleary, *The Struggle for Human Rights*, 145.

35. Paulo Sergio Pinheiro, *Democracia em Pedaços* (São Paulo: Companhia das Letras, 1996), 19.

36. The National Secretariat for Human Rights within the Ministry of Justice was created to promote legislative measures to expand incrimination of human rights abuse. These included reforms of the criminal justice and the judiciary systems, as well as the creation of a federal witness protection program. Also, several state governments initiated local human rights policies.

37. See the Bureau of Democracy, Human Rights, and Labor, U.S. Department of State, "1999 Country Report on Human Rights Practices"; www.state.gov/www/global/human rights/1999/brazil.htm. The report addresses political and other extrajudicial killings, disappearances, tortures, and other cruel, inhuman, or degrading treatment or punishments; arbitrary arrest, detention, or exile; denial of fair public trial; arbitrary interference with privacy, family, home, or correspondence. It also addresses respect for civil and political liberties and discrimination on the basis of race, sex, religion, disability, language, or social status. Information for the report was provided by Amnesty International, Human Rights Watch, and the UN Latin American Institute for Crime Prevention and Treatment of Criminals.

38. The National Indian Foundation has been responsible for Brazilian indigenous policies since 1907. Presently, the indigenous population in Brazil is approximately 300,000, consisting of 210 ethnicities and approximately 170 languages. The majority of the Brazilian indigenous population lives in the midwest and the north. The remaining 40 percent are settled in the northeastern, eastern, and southern regions. The 1988 constitution granted Brazil's indigenous population extensive rights including demarcation of indigenous territory, which should represent approximately 10 percent of the country's territory.

39. According to Brazil's census, 46 percent of the country's population is black (out of a total of 160 million). Yet, estimates suggest that more than 70 percent of Brazil's population is of African ancestry.

40. *Chicago Sun-Times*, August 14, 1994; *Houston Chronicle*, September 18, 1994.

41. An interesting illustration of this kind of reflection is brought up in Eugene Robinson, *Coal to Cream* (New York: Free Press, 1999), where Robinson notes that "it was there [Brazil] that I first really understood that there were other ways to look at race than the way I was accustomed to seeing it, and that some of these ways might involve definitions of race radically different from my own. American society sees race but not color, Brazilian society sees color but not race" (25). A more academic approach to the subject can be found in Peter Fry, "Politics, Nationality, and the Meaning of 'Race' in Brazil," *Daedalus* 129, no. 2 (2000): 83–118.

42. In domestic politics, the 1981 National Environment Policy Act and the 1988 constitution became the backbone of Brazilian environmental policy.

43. See Barry Ames and Margaret Keck, "The Politics of Sustainable Development: Environmental Policy Making in Four Brazilian States," *Journal of Interamerican Studies and World Affairs* 39, no. 4 (1997–98): 1-40.

44. In the last twenty years, Brazil has established a broad set of governmental agencies and secretariats at the municipal, state, and federal levels that have been dedicated to environmental policies. The federal environmental agency, the Brazilian Institute for the Environment and Natural Resources, was established in 1989; the Secretariat of the Environment was created in 1990, and transformed into the Ministry of Environment and Amazon Affairs in 1994, under the administration of Itamar Franco.

45. See Rachel McCleary, "The International Community's Claim to Rights in Brazilian Amazonia," *Political Studies*, no. 39 (1991): 691–707.

46. According to Article 26 of the 1988 Brazilian constitution, the destruction of the Amazonian and Atlantic forests is considered a crime under the penal code.

47. Kathryn Hochstetler, "The Evolution of the Brazilian Environmental Movement and Its Political Roles," in *The New Politics of Inequality in Latin America*, ed. Douglas Chalmers, Carlos Vilas, Katherine Mite, Scott B. Martin, Kevianne Piester, and Monique Segarra (Oxford: Oxford University Press, 1997), 207.

48. Emilio Moran, "The Law, Politics, and Economics of Amazonian Deforestation," *Global Legal Studies Journal*, no. 11 (1988): 1–7.

49. "Environmental Law and Environmental Business Opportunities in Brazil: An Overview"; www.crl.com/~brazil/env.htm.

50. The U.S. government maintains similar meetings with China, India, and Japan.

51. Apart from concerns regarding the destruction of Brazil's Amazon forest, dramatic information has surfaced on the deforestation process of the Atlantic forest, of which only 7 percent is left.

52. The new legislation, submitted by the Ruralist Party in May 2000, would reduce from 80 percent to 50 percent the proportion of the environmental reservation areas. Plus, small properties would not be obliged to replace devastated areas, and legal ecological reserves would be dramatically reduced in economically profitable areas.

53. According to the 1980 U.S. Census, the population of the Brazilian community was slightly greater than 50,000.

54. In 1995, thanks to either institutional support and/or governmental funding, there were 5,497 Brazilian university students in the United States, which led Brazil to rank twelfth among countries of origin of foreign scholars in the country.

55. In the short 1985–88 period, approximately 1,250,000 Brazilians emigrated permanently.

56. Brazilian consulates in the United States are located in Atlanta, Boston, Houston, Miami, New York, San Francisco, and Washington, D.C.

57. In Brazil, the city of Governador Valladares in the state of Minas Gerais has become a paradigmatic example of emigration. Since the early 1980s, there has been a constant flow of immigrants to different parts of the United States.

58. According to the 1990 U.S. Census, the number of Brazilian residents was 94,023. Nevertheless, data collected by the Catholic Archdiocese of Boston in the early 1990s revealed there were 150,000 Brazilians living in Massachusetts alone.

59. As a symbol of the presence of Brazilians in New York City, a section of Forty-sixth Street, where restaurants and stores are owned by Brazilians, has been named "Little Brazil."

60. Wilson Loria, "The Invisible Brazilians"; www.brazil.com.\p25nov99htm.

61. Statement of Jeffrey Davidow, assistant secretary for Inter-American Affairs, U.S. Department of State.

62. Statement of William Perry, president of the Institute for the Study of the Americas. In *Overview of U.S. Policy toward South America and the President's Upcoming Trip to the Region: Hearing before the Subcommittee on the Western Hemisphere.* October 8, 1997, 22.

63. *A Letter to the President and a Memorandum on U.S. Policy toward Brazil: Statement of an Independent Task Force Sponsored by the Council on Foreign Relations,* New York, 2001; www.cfr.org/p/pubs/Brazil.

64. Ibid.

65. Ibid.

66. Ibid.

67. Norah Vincent, "Antidote to the Liberal Monotone," *Los Angeles Times,* April 4, 2002.

68. See chapter 1.

69. Peter Hakim, "Dos maneras de ser global," *Foreign Affairs* (Mexico) 2, no. 1 (2002): 130–44; quote herein is from p. 140.

70. Michael Reynold, Clifford Young, Jamie Shkilnik, and Michael Pergamit, *A Public Opinion Poll on Brazil's Image in the United States of America: Final Report.* National Opinion Research Center at the University of Chicago, April 14, 2000.

71. Referring to the U.S. Trade Representative's critical statement on the subject, the Brazilian health minister replied, "The U.S. Trade Representative is not defending

free trade or free competition. He is only defending the interest of an industry which has enormous influence upon the Bush administration." In this same context President Cardoso gave public declarations that his government would not concede to U.S. pressure.

72. "Entrevista com Helio Jaguaribe," *El Debate Político* (Fondo de Cultura Económica, Buenos Aires,) 1, no. 1 (2003): 95–109.

73. See José Luis Fiori, *60 lições dos 90*, (Rio de Janeiro: Record, 2001).

74. An illustrative evidence of this kind of sentiment was presented in a poll carried forward by the BBC on anti-American feeling about the war against Iraq. The poll surveyed 11,000 people in eleven countries. Brazil was one of the countries in which a negative opinion toward the United States appeared to be the highest. According to the survey, the degree in each country of those interviewed with negative opinions were: Jordan, 79 percent; Brazil, 66 percent; Indonesia, 58 percent; France, 51 percent; Australia, 29 percent; Russia, 28 percent; South Korea, 28 percent; Israel, 25 percent; England, 19 percent; and Canada, 16 percent. "Aversão ao Tio Sam," *Veja*, August 13, 2003.

NOTES FOR CHAPTER 4

1. Luiz Inácio Lula da Silva, a left-wing leader of the Workers Party, was elected president in October 2002.

2. "Brazilians Go Home," *Veja*, January 20, 2003.

3. "A Beleaguered Hemisphere" *New York Times*, November 22, 2002, editorial.

NOTES FOR CHAPTER 5

1. Jeffrey E. Garten, *The Big Ten: The Big Emerging Markets and How They Will Change Our Lives* (New York: Basic Books, 1997), xxv.

2. See Robert Chase, Emily Hill, and Paul Kennedy, eds., *The Pivotal States: A New Framework for U.S. Policy in the Developing World* (New York: Norton, 1999), especially the chapter on Brazil, 165–94.

3. Albert Fishlow, "The United States and Brazil: The Case of the Missing Relationship," *Foreign Affairs* 60, no. 4 (1982): 904–923.

4. See, for example, Kenneth Maxwell, "Avoiding the Imperial Temptation: The United States and Latin America," *World Policy Journal* XVI, no. 3 (1999): 57–67.

5. "A Letter to the President and a Memorandum on U.S. Policy toward Brazil: Statement of an Independent Task Force Sponsored by the Council on Foreign Relations," New York, 2001; www.cfr.org/p/pubs/Brazil.

6. See, for example, the argument of Peter Hakim, "Two Ways to Go Global," *Foreign Affairs* 81, no. 1 (2002): 148–62.

7. For a generally liberal interpretation see Abraham F. Lowenthal, *Partners in Conflict: The United States and Latin America* (Baltimore: Johns Hopkins University

Press, 1987). On the dominance of liberal perspectives see Mark Peceny, "The Inter-American System as a Liberal 'Pacific Union'?" *Latin American Research Review* 29, no. 3 (1994): 188–201. See also Javier Corrales and Richard E. Feinberg, "Regimes of Cooperation in the Western Hemisphere: Power, Interests, and Intellectual Traditions," *International Studies Quarterly*, no. 43 (1999): 1–36.

8. For a clear statement of this view see Andrew Moravcsik, "Liberal International Relations Theory: A Scientific Assessment," in *Progress in International Relations Theory*, ed. Colin Elman and Miriam Fendius Elman (Cambridge, Mass.: MIT Press, 2002).

9. As the then U.S. ambassador put it, "'The United States played no role in abertura. In the period of time that I was in Brazil, 1981 through 1984, I always counseled Washington, and for once they took my advice, that abertura ["opening" or political liberalization] was made in Brazil, and both from a public and private posture the United States was better off staying out of it. The Brazilians defined what abertura was and what the timetable was to be. All we did was applaud the process.'" See Langhore A. Motley, "Letting Off Steam," in *Authoritarian Regimes in Transition*, ed. Hans Binnendijk (Washington, D.C.: Foreign Service Institute, 1987), 250.

10. Marcílio Marques Moreira, *Diplomacia, Política e Fianças*, ed. Dora Rocha and Alexandra de Mello e Silva (Rio de Janeiro: Editora Objetiva, 2001), 155; my translation.

11. Fernando Henrique Cardoso, address at the opening session of Third Summit of the Americas, Quebec City, April 20, 2002; http://www.brazil.org.uk.

12. For the most thorough account, see David Malone, *Decision-Making in the UN Security Council: The Case of Haiti, 1990–1997* (Oxford: Clarendon Press, 1998), especially 83–112.

13. For a discussion of the evolving debates on democracy, see Laurence Whitehead, *Democratization: Theory and Experience* (Oxford: Oxford University Press, 2002), chapter 1, "On 'Democracy' and 'Democratization.'"

14. On the importance of informal processes of WTO decision making, see Amrita Narlikar, "The Politics of Participation: Decision-Making Processes and Developing Countries in the World Trade Organization," *Round Table*, no. 364 (2002): 171–85. On Brazilian trade policy, see Ricardo Caldas, *Brazil in the Uruguay Round of the GATT* (Aldershot, England: Ashgate, 1998).

15. There are, of course, other elements to the strategic role of MERCOSUR for Brazil: integration as a means of taking forward a national industrial project under new global conditions, of attracting foreign capital and direct foreign investment, and of overcoming the previously costly and dangerous insecurity generated by rivalry with Argentina.

16. We should also remember that such calculations appear to have played only a very small role in other economic regionalist projects in both Europe and beyond. Negotiators have often relied on very crude and imprecise estimates of likely costs and benefits, and politics has tended to dominate. See Sheila Page, *Regionalism among Developing Countries* (Basingstoke, England: Macmillan, 2000).

17. Fernando Henrique Cardoso, address at the opening session of Third Summit of the Americas, Quebec City, April 20, 2002; http://www.brazil.org.uk.

18. See, for example, Princeton N. Lyman, "The Growing Influence of Domestic Factors," in *Multilateralism and U.S. Foreign Policy: Ambivalent Engagement*, ed. Stewart Patrick and Shepard Foreman (Boulder, Colo.: Lynne Rienner, 2002). On the region see, in particular, the writings of Abraham Lowenthal.

19. See, for example, Maxwell A. Cameron and Brian W. Tomlin, *The Making of NAFTA: How the Deal Was Done* (Ithaca, N.Y.: Cornell University Press, 2000), where it is noted that according to "the estimate by a senior U.S. official . . . over the course of the fast-track proceedings and the actual NAFTA negotiations, the American negotiating team held more than four hundred meetings with members of Congress and staffers, and between twelve thousand and sixteen thousand meetings with the private sector" (230).

20. For one of the clearest discussions, see G. John Ikenberry, David A. Lake, and Michael Mastanduno, eds., *The State and American Foreign Economic Policy* (Ithaca, N.Y.: Cornell University Press, 1998).

21. Robert Putnam, "Diplomacy and Domestic Politics. The Logic of Two-Level Games," in *Double-Edged Diplomacy*, ed. Peter B. Evans, Harold K. Jacobsen and Robert D. Putnam (Berkeley and Los Angeles: University of California Press, 1993), 450. Compare the extent to which the NAFTA negotiations confirmed this prediction: "A number of Mexican negotiators stessed that their decision-making power was both an asset and a liability. In the words of one, 'Our greatest strength was also our greatest weakness: we could decide a lot. But we could not say "Congress won't like this," or even "the industry won't accept this."'" Cameron and Tomlin, *The Making of NAFTA*, 230.

22. Daniel Deudney and G. John Ikenbery, "Realism, Structural Liberalism, and the Western Order," in *Unipolar Politics: Realism and State Strategies after the Cold War*, ed. Ethan B. Kapstein and Michael Mastanduno (New York: Columbia University Press, 1999), 109–10. See also G. John Ikenberry, *After Victory: Institutions, Strategic Restraint and the Rebuilding of Order after Major Wars* (Princeton, N.J.: Princeton University Press, 2001).

23. See Miles Kahler, ed., *Liberalization and Foreign Policy* (New York: Columbia University Press, 1997).

24. For discussions of interest-group activity in foreign trade policy, see Jeffrey Casson, "Democracy Looks South: Mercosur and the Politics of Brazilian Trade Strategy," in *Democratic Brazil: Actors, Institutions and Processes*, ed. Peter R. Kingstone and Timothy J. Power (Pittsburgh: Mercosur, 2000); Ben Ross Schneider, "Business Politics and Regional Integration: The Advantages of Organization in NAFTA and Mercosur," in *Regional Integration in Latin America and the Caribbean: The Political Economy of Open Regionalism*, ed. Victor Bulmer-Thomas (London: ILAS, 2001). More generally, see Kurt Weyland, "The Fragmentation of

Business in Brazil," in *Organized Business, Economic Change, and Democracy in Latin America,* ed. Francisco Durand and Eduardo Silva (Miami: North South Center Press, 1998).

25. Maria Regina Soares de Lima, "Instituições Democráticas e Política Exterior," *Contexto Internacional* 22, no. 2 (2000): 265–303.

26. See Margaret E. Keck and Kathryn Sikkink, *Activists beyond Borders: Advocacy Networks in International Politics* (Ithaca, N.Y.: Cornell University Press, 1998).

27. Three perennial questions arise when faced with claims about the importance of transnational civil society groups: Exactly how transnational is the civil society, as opposed to being a matter of domestic political pluralism? How autonomous is it from the state? How precisely, do such groups matter, and to whom?

28. Roberto Patricio Koreniewiecz and William C. Smith, "Transnational Social Movements, Elite Projects, and Collective Action from Below in the Americas," in *Regionalism and Governance in the Americas,* eds. L. Fawcett and M. Serrano (New York: Palgrave, forthcoming).

29. On the importance of unevenness, see Laurence Whitehead, "Bowling in the Bronx: The Uncivil Interstices between Civil and Political Society," *Democratization* 4, no. 1 (1997): 12.

30. Ngaire Woods, "Order, Justice, the IMF and World Bank" in *Order and Justice in International Relations,* ed. Rosemary Foot, John Gaddis, and Andrew Hurrell (Oxford: Oxford University Press, 2003), 99–101.

31. See Ann M Florini, ed., *The Third Force: The Rise of Transnational Civil Society* (Washington, D.C.: Carnegie Endowment, 2000).

32. Maria Rita Loureiro and Gilberto Tadeu Lima, "A Internacionalização da Ciência Econômica no Brasil," *Revista de Economia Política* 14, no. 3 (1994): 31–50. The weakness of a liberal tradition is also highlighted in Luis Carlos Bresser Pereira, "Seis Interpretações Sôbre O Brasil" *Dados* 25, no. 3 (1982): 269–306.

33. Loureiro and Lima, "A Internacionalização," 48; my translation.

34. For critiques, see, for example, Paulo Nogueira Batista Jr., *A Economia com ela É,* 2nd ed. (São Paulo: Boitempo Editorial, 2001), especially chapters 1 and 2; and Geisa Maria Rocha, "Neo-Dependency in Brazil," *New Left Review,* no. 16 (2002): 5–33. For a defense, see Gustavo Franco, "A inserção externa e o desenvolvimento," *Revista de Economia Política,* no. 3 (1998): 121–147.

35. Rubens Barbosa, "Existe America Latina?" *Folha de São Paulo,* March 5, 2003.

36. Fernando Henrique Cardoso, "Relações Norte-Sul no Contexto Atual: Uma Nova Dependência," in *O Brasil e a Economia Global,* ed. Renato Baumann (Rio de Janeiro: Editora Campus, 1996), 10; my translation.

37. Ibid., 12.

38. For a firsthand account, see Moreira, *Diplomacia,* 223–69; and the analysis in Maria Regina Soares de Lima and Mônica Hirst, "O Brasil e os Estados Unidos: Delams e Desafios de uma Relação Complexa," in *Temas de Política Externa Brasileira II,*

ed. Gélson Fonseca and Sérgio Henrique Nabuco de Castro (Rio de Janeiro: Paz e Terra, 1994), 58–59.

39. See Celso Lafer's speech of August 2, 2002, A *Palavra Internacional do Brasil,* August 8, 2002.

40. Tony Judt, "Its Own Worst Enemy," *New York Review of Books,* August 15, 2002, 13.

41. For a collection of Brazilian reactions to the events of September 11, 2001, and a U.S. view of their origins, see Kenneth Maxwell, "Anti-Americanism in Brazil," *Correspondence: An International Review of Culture and Society,* no. 9 (2002); http://www.cfr.org/pdf/correspondence/xMaxwell.php.

42. On the common assumption that outsiders do not need to study the United States because "we all know it already," see François Heisbourg, "American Hegemony? Perceptions of the U.S. Abroad," *Survival* 41, no. 4 (1999–2000): 5–19.

43. For the classic discussion, see Robert Jervis, *Perception and Misperception in International Politics* (Princeton, N.J.: Princeton University Press, 1976).

44. These are the questions that have driven much recent constructivist research on norms, culture, and identity. See, in particular, Peter J. Katzenstein, "Introduction," in *The Culture of National Security,* ed. Peter J. Katzenstein (New York: Columbia University Press, 1996).

45. José Murilo de Carvalho, "'Dreams Come Untrue,'" *Daedalus* 129, no. 2 (2000): 68. Special issue entitled "Brazil: Burden of the Past; Promise of the Future."

46. The literature on the external sources of Brazilian preferences is underdeveloped. For a recent analysis of the United States that stresses both the importance of the external and the success of state building, see Ira Katznelson and Martin Shefter, eds., *Shaped by War and Trade: International Influences on American Political Development* (Princeton, N.J.: Princeton University Press, 2002).

47. Luiz Inácio Lula da Silva, speech, Brasilia, March 17, 2003, A *Palavra Internacional do Brasil,* March 20, 2003; my translation.

48. Pew Research Center, *What the World Thinks in 2002: The Pew Global Attitudes Project* (Washington, D.C.: Pew Research Center, 2002), 48. The survey also highlighted the strong Brazilian view that the United States did not take into account the interests of others (59), and also that its actions work to increase the gap between rich and poor (61).

49. Marco Aurelio Garcia, interview, *Época,* March 24, 2003; my translation.

Abertura, 118
Acquired immunodeficiency
    syndrome (AIDS),
    31, 105
Action Plan for Human
    Rights, 54
Adjustment, xvi, 10–11
Affirmative posture, xvi
African ancestry, 114
Afro-Brazilian organizations, 55
Agricultural products, 27
    Brazil, 27
    subsidization, 31
Agriculture, 106
AIDS, 31, 105
Albright, Madeleine K., 112
Alignment, xvi, 5–8
Alliance, xvi, 1–5
Alliance for Progress, 7
Amazon region's Calha Norte
    Project, 47
Amazon Surveillance
    System, 113
American Common Market, 34
Amil, 24
Amnesty International, 80, 88
Amnesty Law, 52
Andean Pact, 34
Anglophone Caribbean, ix
Angola
    UN Mission, 43
Antagonistic confrontation, 65
Antidrug Secretariat, 49,
    113n21
Antidumping duties, 110
    steel imports, 29
Anti-interventionist
    foreign policy, 46
Anti-Soviet diplomacy, 5

Aranha, Oswaldo, 4
Argentina, 45, 93
    Brazilian relations, 40
    democratization, ix
    full-scope alignment with
        United States, 40
    strident pro-Americanism, 95
Asymmetric power
    structure, 40
Autonomous policy, xvi
Autonomy, 8–10
Autonomy-driven
    confrontation, 65
Axis of evil, 102
Azevedo da Silveira,
    Francisco, 8

Bahia, 55
Balance and perspectives,
    67–71
Bandwagoning with United
    States, 99
Bank for International
    Recovery and
    Development (BIRD), 6
Beltway politics, 86
Bilateral Working Group for
    Defense, 44
BIRD, 6
Bolivia
    cocaine, xi
Brazil. See also specific topics
    agricultural products, 27
    anti-Soviet diplomacy, 5
    characteristics, 73
    democratization, ix
    diversity of ecosystems and
        environmental
        challenges, 57

direct interactions with
    United States, 82
manufactured products, 28
public debt, 24
steel producers, 28–29
U.S. exports, 28t
U.S. imports, 27t
USFDI, 22, 23t
Brazilian Antidrug Secretariat,
    49, 113n21
Brazilian community
    Brazilian consulates
        locations, 116
Brazilian Defense Ministry, 44
Brazilian exports, 3
Brazilian Foreign Ministry, 51
Brazilian foreign policy
    vs. other Latin American
        states, 74–75
Brazilian government
    U.S. view, 96
Brazilian Green Party, 57
Brazilian immigration
    to United States, 59–60
Brazilian NGOs, 59
Brazilian products, 92
Brazilian Workers Party,
    57, 76
Brazil's Diplomatic Academy, 56
Brazil's economic
    development, 4
Bridge builder, 81
Burns, Bradford, 1
Bush, George H.W., x, xii, 32
Bush, George W., 59
Bush administration, 70

CACM, viii
Canadian government, 89

Cardoso, Fernando Henrique, 11, 75, 77, 119
Cardoso administration, 69, 80, 83, 92–94, 102
  FTAA negotiations, 38
Caribbean, 85
Caribbean Community (CARICOM), viii
CARICOM, viii
Carter, Jimmy, 8, 52
Castro, Fidel, 70, 102
CDM, 58
Central America
  civil war termination, x
Central American Common Market (CACM), viii
Centrality of U.S. power, 107
Chávez, Hugo, 102, 104
  coup against, 79
  democratic principles, 70
Chile, 70, 90, 96
  democratization, ix
China, 91, 102
Citrosuco, 24
Citrus crops
  Florida and Brazil, 28
Civil war termination
  Central America, x
Clean Development Mechanism (CDM), 58
Clinton, Bill, x, xii, 11, 32, 112
Clinton administration, 82
Clinton years, 58
Cocaine
  international organized crime, xi
  U.S. consumption, xi
Cold War, x
  beginning of, 5
  effect on U.S.-Brazil relations, xv, 95
  end of
    in Brazil, 43
    economic exposure, 10, 64
    environment, 56
    in Europe, x
    liberalism, 75
    national interest, 85
    perceived globalization intensification, 74
    technologically driven globalization, 93–94
  impact directly on Brazil, 98–99
  impact on economic policy, xi
  military alliances, 48
  overlap, 99
  post-era, 40–42

institutions, 79
U.S. globalization vision, 65
Collor de Mello, Fernando, 10, 11, 19, 94, 95, 99
Colombia, 70, 104, 107
  cocaine, xi
  military, xii
Colombian government, 47
Colombia Plan, 112
Commercial transactions, 20
Comparative reflections, 73–107
Complexity of country, 96
Condescending indifference U.S., 97
Constrained discrepancy, xv
Council on Foreign Relations, 61–62
Cuba, 107
  OAS sanctions, 77
Cuban Missile Crisis, 7
Culture
  U.S. role, xi
Currency, 21
Cutrale, 24

Davos, 102
DEA, 49
Defense matters, 47
Deficit
  Brazil
    U.S. vs. neighbors, 34
Democracy
  challenges facing changing nature, 78
Democracy Summit, 77
Democratization, ix, 77
  Argentina, ix
Density
  economic, ecological, societal interdependence, 90
Department of Commerce, 19
Department of the Treasury, 19
Dependency-style analyses, 93
Depth
  economic, ecological, societal interdependence, 90
Devaluation, 26
Dispute settlements
  U.S.-Brazil, 30t
Divergent perceptions, 97
Doha meeting, 31
Doha Trade Round, 102
Domestic economic coalitions, 87
Domestic economics, 21–24
Domestic political regimes, ix

Drug Enforcement Administration (DEA) 49
Drug trafficking, 41, 49

Earth Summit, 57
East Timor
  UN peace operation, 43
Economic development, 4
Economic interdependence levels, 85, 91
Economic issues, 7
Economic reform
  Brazil's "laggard" status, 95, 96
Economic relations, 19–38
Economic stabilization, 11
Economic transformation, vii
Ecosystems
  diversity of, 57
Ecuador, 82
Ecuador-Peru peace process, 41
Eisenhower, Dwight D., 6
Electing opposition candidate Mexicans, ix
Elections, Latin American, ix
El Salvador
  UN Observer Mission, 43
Embraco, 24
Embraer, 24
Emigration
  to United States, 60
Environment, 56–59
Environmental challenges, 57
European Union (EU), 80
Eximbank, 6

Fast-track negotiating authority, 34, 36, 46, 83, 85, 111, 119
Fernando de Noronha, 6
Fifth Defense Ministerial, 48
Figueiredo, João, 9
Financial assistance package, 110
First Republic, 2
  positive bilateral relations, 3
First World, 95
Fishlow, Albert, 73
Florida
  citrus crops, 28
Foreign Ministry, 19, 41
Foreign policy, 102
  anti-interventionist, 46
  direction and tenor, 101
  economic, 85–87
  vs. other Latin American states, 74–75
  in relation to United States. See United States

Fourth Defense Ministerial
    Conference of the
    Americas, 48
Fox, Vincente, ix
Franco, Itamar, 11
Free Trade Agreement for the
    Americas (FTAA), 21,
    32, 33, 34, 68, 75,
    82–84, 87, 103, 104,
    106, 107
    negotiating process, 35–36
    preparatory phases, 35
    and trade integration, 88–89
Free Trade Area, 83
Fruit and vegetable imports
    U.S., 27t
FTAA. See Free Trade
    Agreement for the
    Americas
Fujimori, Alberto, ix, xii, 77

GATT, 30, 87
GDP. See Gross domestic
    product
Geisel, Ernesto, 8
General Agreement on Tariffs
    and Trade (GATT),
    30, 87
General System Preference, 27
Gerdau, 24
German influence
    in Brazil, 3
Germany, 58
Global economy
    Brazil, 90–91
Global financial turmoil, 20
Global insecurity, 105
Global security threats
    approaches, 42
Good neighbor policy, 3
Gorbachev, Mikhail, x
Goulart, João, 5, 7
Green market, 58
Grenada, ix
Gross domestic product
    (GDP), 92
    growth rates (1996–1998),
    110
Group of Friends of Venezuela,
    70, 104
Growth rates
    economic miracle, 100
Guatemala, ix
Guyana, ix

Haiti, ix, 77
    crisis, 40
Hakim, Peter, 62
Harrington, Anthony, 110

Hegemonic presumption, 101
Hemispheric defense
    conference, 48
Hemispheric free trade, xii
Hemispheric Free Trade
    Agreement, 38, 46
Hills, Carla, 111
Hobbesian analytic
    liberalism, 76
Hrinak, Donna, 68
Human rights, 51–56
    abuses, 53, 54
    refocusing and retrenchment,
    52–54
    violations
        high-level agents, 78
Human Rights Watch of the
    Americas, 53, 80, 88

IATW, 58
IDB, 57, 82
Ideological liberalism, 76–79
IFI, 91, 95
IMF, 20, 87
Immigration
    to United States, 59–60
Imperial unilateralism, 65
Import substitution
    industrialization (ISI),
    90–91
Independent Foreign Policy, 7
India, 91, 102
Inflation rates
    1994–1998, 110
Initiative of the Americas, 33
Insider activism, 80
Insider networks, 89
Institutions
    effect on U.S.-Brazil
    relations, 79–85
Interagency coordination, 113
Inter-American Development
    Bank (IDB), 57, 82
Inter-American System, 5
Inter-American Treaty of
    Reciprocal Assistance,
    5, 42
International Agreement for
    Tropical Woods
    (IATW), 58
International Atomic Energy
    Agency safeguards, 79
International Covenant on
    Civil and Political
    Rights, 80
International environmental
    organization, 57
International financial
    institutions (IFI), 91, 95

International migration, xi
International Monetary Fund
    (IMF), 20, 87
International organized crime
    cocaine, xi
International regulations, 29
Interstate political
    relations, 40
Ioschpe, 24
Ipope, 24
ISI, 90–91
Itamaraty, 41

Joint Initiative for the
    Environment at the UN
    General Assembly, 58
Judt, Tony, 97

Kennedy, John F., 7
Kissinger, Henry, 8, 62, 99
Koreniewiecz, Roberto
    Patricio, 89
Kosovo tragedy, 40
Kubitschek, Juscelino, 6
Kyoto Conference on Climate
    Change, 58
Kyoto Protocol, 58, 59

Lampreia, Luiz Felipe, 112
Lamy, Pascal, 103
Language, 102
Latin American and Caribbean
    conference, 47
Latin American
    convergence, 91
Latin American economic and
    political loyalty, 3
Latin American states
    vs. Brazilian foreign policy,
    74–75
Latinos, 60
Law of National Security, 52
Liberal perspectives
    U.S.–Latin America
    relations, 76
Lima, Gilberto Tadeu, 90
Loureiro, Maria Rita, 90
Lula da Silva, Luiz Inácio,
    24, 75
    implications of election,
    101–107

Machiavelli, Niccolò, 98
Malgalhães, Juracy, 7
Manufactured products, 28
    Brazil, 28
Marx, Karl, 98
Memorandum of
    Understanding, 49

Mercado Comun del Cono Sur
    (MERCOSUR), viii, 10,
    11, 21, 32, 33, 34,
    37–38, 45, 48, 69, 75,
    81, 82, 83, 86, 103
    strategic role, 118
MERCOSUR. *See* Mercado
    Comun del Cono Sur
Mexico, 70, 85, 86, 90, 91,
    92, 107
    electing opposition
        candidate, ix
    freedom, 106
    political parties, x
    U.S. interests, 84
Miami Summit, 84
Migration
    to United States, 60
Military, xii
    Colombian conflict, 104
    cooperation, 6
Millennium Trade Round, 81
Ministry of Agriculture, 19
Ministry of Development, 19
Ministry of Economy, 19
Misperceptions
    danger, 97
Missile Technology Control
    Regime, 11, 42, 79
Moreira, Marcílio Marques, 77
Most Favored Nation status, 4
Movement of the Landless, 55
Mozambique
    UN Observer Mission, 43
Multilateral institutionalism, 20
Multilateral organizations, 52
Multilateral trade system, 31
Mutual Legal Assistance
    Treaty, 49

Nabuco, Joaquim, 2
NAFTA. *See* North American
    Free Trade Agreement
Narcotics agreement, 49
National Drug Control
    Policy, 49
National Indian Foundation, 114
National Opinion Research
    Center (NORC), 63
Neoliberal economic
    ideas, 90
NGO. *See* Nongovernmental
    organizations
Nixon Doctrine, 99
Nongovernmental
    organizations (NGO),
    50, 88–89, 103
    Global Forum, 102
Nonlicensed pharmaceuticals, 31

NORC, 63
North American Free Trade
    Agreement (NAFTA),
    viii, 21, 30, 83, 84
    costs and benefits, 35
NSC, 89
Nuclear Non-Proliferation
    Treaty, 11, 79
Nuclear program, 8
Nuclear Suppliers Group, 79
Nuclear technology, 44–45

OAS. *See* Organization of
    American States
Odebrecht, 24
Old south, 94
Orange juice, 28
Organization for Economic
    Cooperation and
    Development, 81
Organization of American
    States (OAS), 5, 70,
    82, 97
    conference, 42
    Drug Abuse Control
        Commission, 49
    sanctions, 77

Pan-American Operation, 6
Paraguay, ix, 45
    democratic government, 77
    democratic transition, 41
Pastrana, Andres, 112
Pattern explanation
    U.S.-Brazil relations,
    75–76
Patterson, Richard, 95
Perceptions, 94
    and public opinion, 60–65
Persian Gulf War, 10, 40
Peru, ix, 82
    cocaine, xi
    military, xii
    OAS sanctions, 77
Petrobras, 24
Pinto, Magalhães, 7
Pivotal regional players, 99
Plan Colombia, 84
    hemispheric defense
        conference, 48
Pluralism and foreign policy,
    85–87
Political maturity, 60
Political parties
    Mexico, x
Political support, 6
Portugal, 70
Power maximizing state
    Brazil, 99

Power state, 100
Practical political action, 99
Presidential Summit,
    45–46
Public debt, 24
Public opinion, 60–65

Quadros, Jânio, 5, 7
Querari Operation, 47
Quito Ministerial Meeting, 104

Rawls, John, 77
Reagan, Ronald, 95
Real Plan, 11, 21, 25, 81
Regional economic agenda, 104
Regional policies and security,
    45–50
Regionwide economic
    change, viii
Relations with United States
    chronology, 12–18
    economic, 19–38
Revisionist state, 100
Rezek, Francisco, 80
Rio Branco, Barão de, 1–2
    Foreign Ministry, 2–3
Rio Branco Academy, 56
Rio de Janeiro Conference
    (1947), 5
Rio de Janeiro 1992 Earth
    Summit, 79
Robinson, Eugene, 115
Romi, 24
Ruralist Party, 115
Russia, 91

SAFTA, 34, 81
Santiago Summit, 36
Sarney, José, 9
September 11, 2001, 68, 69
    Brazilian reactions, 42, 97, 121
Seventh United Nations
    Conference on Climate
    Change, 59
Singapore, 58
Smith, William C., 89
South Africa, 58, 102
South American Free Trade
    Area (SAFTA), 34, 81
Southern Cone Common
    Market. *See* Mercado
    Comun del Cono Sur
South Korea, 86
Soviet Union, x
Spain, 70
State power, 89
Steel imports
    antidumping duties, 29
Steel producers, 28–29

Tariffs, 27
  exemptions or
    reductions, 109
Technocrat democratic
    revolution, 94
Tequila crisis, 34
Third Hemispheric
    Presidential Summit, 36
Third Ministerial Conference, 90
TPA, 36–38, 83, 85, 105
Trade Act of 1974, 109
Trade agenda, 9
Trade imbalance
  with United States, 34
Trade promotion authority
    (TPA), 36–38, 83,
    85, 105
Trade Related Aspects of
    Intellectual Property
    Rights (TRIPS), 31
Trading state, 100
Transnational advocacy
    networks, 50, 113
Transnational civil society,
    87–90
Treaty of Asunción, 32
Treaty of Tlatelolco, 79
Treaty on Conventional
    Weapons, 11
Triple border area, 48
TRIPS, 31
Truman, Harry, 6

Ungoverned spaces, 104
United Nations Drug Control
    Program, 49
United Nations Forest
    Fora, 58
United Nations General
    Assembly, 43
  resolutions on disarmament
    and human rights, 43t
United Nations Human Rights
    Commission, 54
United Nations Mission
  Angola, 43
United Nations Observer
    Mission
  El Salvador, 43
  Mozambique, 43
United Nations peacekeeping
    operations, 43
  East Timor, 43
United Nations Security
    Council (UNSC)
  expansion, 44

United Nations World
    Conference against
    Racism, Discrimination
    and Related
    Intolerance, 56
United States
  cocaine consumption, xi
  Colombia security
    priorities, 70
  culture, role of, xi
  domestic politics, 86
  exports to Brazil, 27t
  fruit and vegetable
    imports, 27t
  German rivalry
    Brazilian foreign affairs, 3
  Latin America
    convergence of values and
    interests, 82
    relations, viii
  Mexico relations, 62
  tariff rate quota system, 27
  view of Brazil
    as economic "laggard,"
    95–96
    war on terrorism, 96–97
United States and Brazil
  dispute settlements, 30t
  relations, xv
    chronology, 12–18
    economic, 19–38
    historical background,
      1–18
    ideology, role of, 76–79
    institutions, role of
      acceptance, 79–85
    limitations and caveats,
      94–101
    multilateral dimension,
      29–32
    pluralism and foreign
      policy, 85–87
    political, 39–65
    regional dimension,
      32–33
    transnational civil society,
      role of, 88
  trade, 24–29, 25t
  surplus, 26
United States Census, 116
United States Council on
    Foreign Relations Task
    Force Report, 74
United States Drug
    Enforcement
    Administration, 49

United States Export and Import
    Bank (Eximbank), 6
United States foreign direct
    investment (USFDI)
    1998, 22t
United States International
    Trade Commission
    (USITC), 29
United States Trade
    Representative (USTR),
    85, 105, 116–118
UNSC
  expansion, 44
Unwritten alliance, 1
Uruguay, 81, 83
  democratization, ix
USAID, 89
USFDI
    1998, 22t
USITC, 29
USTR, 85, 105, 116–118

Vale do Rio Doce, 24
Vargas, Getúlio, 3
Venezuela, 45, 104, 107
  military, xii
Vienna Human Rights
    Conference, 81
Voice opportunities, 80

War on Iraq, 106
War on terrorism, 96–97, 106
Washington Agreement
    (1942), 5
Wasmosy, Juan Carlos, 45
Whitehead, Laurence, 89
Woods, Ngaire, 90
Workers Party, 24, 103
World Bank, 20, 57
World Conference of Human
    Rights, 54
World politics and security,
    42–45
World satellite launching
    industry, 112
World Summit on Sustainable
    Development in South
    Africa, 59
World Trade Organization
    (WTO), 20, 29, 31, 81,
    87, 105
  Dispute Settlement
    Procedures, 80
World War II, 4

Zoellick, Robert B., 37